THE BOOK OF JOE

ALSO BY JEFF WILSER

Alexander Hamilton's Guide to Life

*The Good News About What's Bad for You . . .
and the Bad News About What's Good for You*

The Maxims of Manhood

THE
BOOK
OF
JOE

THE LIFE, WIT, AND (SOMETIMES ACCIDENTAL) WISDOM OF

═ JOE BIDEN ═

JEFF WILSER

THREE RIVERS PRESS
NEW YORK

All rights reserved.
Published in the United States by Three Rivers Press,
an imprint of the Crown Publishing Group,
a division of Penguin Random House LLC, New York.
crownpublishing.com

Three Rivers Press and the Tugboat design
are registered trademarks of Penguin Random House LLC.

Library of Congress Cataloging-in-Publication Data
is available upon request.

ISBN 978-0-525-57258-9
Ebook ISBN 978-0-525-57259-6

PRINTED IN THE UNITED STATES OF AMERICA

Book design by Andrea Lau
Illustrations by Mark Stutzman
Cover design by Alane Gianetti
Photographs on pages 15 and 16 courtesy of Branden Brooks
Cover photograph by SERGEI SUPINSKY/Staff/AFP/Getty Images

10 9 8 7 6 5 4 3 2 1

First Edition

Failure at some point in your life is inevitable,
but giving up is unforgivable.

—JOE BIDEN

CONTENTS

═ INTRODUCTION ═

2008. TALLAHASSEE. JOE BIDEN HAD been campaigning all day, most of it on his feet. Talking, laughing, joking, hugging, Biden-ing. He had to be exhausted. Finally, at dusk, his weary team slogged back to the airport. Time to rest, recharge.

As they pulled up to the tarmac, Biden noticed a group of kids, Cub Scouts, who were there to visit a fire truck.

Hey, he thought, *Cub Scouts!*

Revitalized, Biden ran over and shook their hands, hugged them, tousled hair. Then he had an idea. "You guys wanna come and see my plane?"

"Yeah!" the kids cried out.

"Is it okay?" Biden asked a staffer, like a teenager asking to borrow the family car. The staffer gave the thumbs-up.

YES! After getting permission from their (amazed) parents, Biden walked the kids to his plane, where his wife, Jill, cheerfully waved them on board. Joe showed them the cockpit, gave them a grand tour, and learned their names along the way, almost as if he were charming a prime minister.

One of the kids spotted a basket of candy. "Is that your snacks?"

"That's our snacks," Biden said, then lowered his voice to a whisper. "You can sneak one if you want." He doled out some Tootsie Rolls. "Everybody got one?"

His assistant at the time, Herbie Ziskend, remembers the day well. "These little kids were adorable. And he met them all." This wasn't a campaign event. This wasn't scripted or planned. Biden just loves this kind of stuff. The best part? "The kids didn't know who he was!" Ziskend says, laughing.

It seems that everyone who has worked with Biden, knows Biden, or once bumped into him on the Amtrak has a favorite story to share. Like the Delaware woman who says he raced down a thief to save her purse, the neighbor who watched him zip around in his Corvette, or the teenager who met Biden once, just once, but received some advice that would help him conquer a speech impediment. Colleagues and staffers can vouch for that authenticity, that warmth, how he's the same Joe whether the camera is on or off . . . for better or worse.

Just ask the cameraman. "He's almost *exactly* the same," says Arun Chaudhary, the nation's first-ever White House videographer, whose team shadowed Biden and President Obama, capturing their every moment, whether they were talking policy or licking ice cream cones.

Or, as Obama put it, "Folks don't just feel like they know Joe 'the politician.' They feel like they know the person. What makes him laugh, what he believes, what he cares about, where he came from. Pretty much every time he speaks, he treats us to some wisdom from the nuns who taught him in grade school."

The goal of this book is to unpack that wisdom—not just the lessons from the sisters at Holy Rosary, but the hard-fought insights he has earned from a lifetime of service. Biden has freely, *gleefully*, shared much of this advice in countless speeches, interviews, and gabfests with students, but no one has really collected it all in one place. So throughout the book you'll find callouts to the "Wisdom of Joe," little dollops of insight that apply to us all.

Why Joe Biden? The premise is simple: Biden is a good man; Biden is *the* man. We can learn from the way he speaks plainly, stays upbeat, and treats others with respect, no matter who they are or how they vote. That basic *decency* is why liking Joe Biden is a nonpartisan issue. His pals have ranged from liberal lions (Ted Kennedy) to arch conservatives (Strom Thurmond). "If you can't admire Joe Biden as a person, you've got a problem," suggests Republican Lindsey Graham in his slow, southern drawl. "He is as good a man as God ever created."

"Joe Biden doesn't have a mean bone in his body," says John McCain. "He's unique in that he's had some role in every major national security crisis that his nation has faced in the last thirty-five years. I don't know anyone like him in the U.S. Senate. . . . I would say he's been the most impactful vice president that I've known—certainly in modern times."

McCain has a good point—Biden isn't just a "nice guy"; he also gets things done. When we take stock of Joe's legacy, we see a record of service that has few modern-day parallels. Who else pushed to end wars in both Vietnam *and* Iraq? Who else worked with eight presidents, from Nixon to Obama? (Or as he put it, "Folks, I can tell you I've known eight presidents, three of them intimately.") As chairman of the Robert Bork proceedings, he might have done more to shape the Supreme Court than anyone since FDR. He championed the Violence Against Women Act. Pushed through a crime bill that put 100,000 cops on the street. Fought to end the genocide in Bosnia. And he did all that before he became, in Obama's totally unbiased judgment, "the best vice president America's ever had."

Why this book? Let's not kid ourselves. An entire generation knows

Biden mostly from the aviators, the Amtrak, the "bromance" memes, and the ice cream cones. And, okay, the gaffes. In an odd way, we only embraced Joe Biden *after* he left the White House, sort of like how we might not appreciate an ex until after the breakup.

So another mission of the book is to give Joe his due, to look back on his life and savor the best nuggets. As should be clear from the cover, this is not an academic tome or a year-by-year account of Biden's life, from birth to Air Force Two. (For that, I recommend Jules Witcover's exceptionally well-researched 2010 biography, *Joe Biden: A Life of Trial and Redemption,* as well as Biden's own 2007 memoir, *Promises to Keep.*) Instead, the goal here is to offer something that can be binged in a single weekend, focusing on the key stories and lessons from Biden's remarkable life and career.

Why now? Or, to be as blunt as Biden, isn't this old news? Shouldn't we be looking forward, not backward?

First off, Joe's wisdom is timeless. And it can be helpful to look at the past—the good and the bad, the wins and the misfires. Joe Biden isn't perfect; that's the price of being a public servant for nearly five decades. (Quick perspective: When Biden prepared to launch his first campaign, the Yankees were led by a player named Mickey Mantle.) So the book doesn't pretend the flaws don't exist; instead we'll look at those missteps and suss out the teachable moments.

Most important, we can learn from the way that Biden, time after time, has bounced back from unthinkable tragedy and heartache. As his longtime right-hand man, former senator Ted Kaufman, once said, "If you ask me, who is the luckiest person I have ever known? I would say Joe Biden. If you ask me, who is the unluckiest I have known? I would say Joe Biden." As a young man he lost his first wife and baby daughter. As an old man he lost his son. Along the way he nearly died from a brain aneurysm, with a priest giving him last rites. That's why when Biden says something like, "I feel your pain," it's not phony. With Biden it's real. He does feel the pain, and he has felt the sharp edges of that pain for more than forty years.

Yet this is what makes Joe, well, Joe: Through it all, he carries himself with grace and strength, and somehow, against all odds, he even finds a way to see the *humor*. The tears are followed by a smile, a chuckle, some finger-guns. In fact, he is so effective at exuding this breezy cool, this *Ah, Shucks* friendliness, that at times we forget that he is a man of substance and grit, a man who has a knack for bucking the odds, for coming back from the brink.

Joe's comebacks began in the very beginning. When Biden was a boy, then just "Joey," after any setback, his father would tell him, *Get back up! Get up! Get up!* He has followed that advice as a child, as a man, and as a father.

None of us have walked in Biden's shoes or faced the same tragedies, but all of us will know loss, feel heartache, suffer bruising defeats. As just one example, on November 8, 2016, about 65.8 million Americans were knocked to the floor by a sucker punch.

Joe can help us get back up.

PART I

THE UPSTART

The Boy Who Couldn't Speak (1942–60)

"I may be Irish, but I'm not stupid."

ACROSS THE POLITICAL SPECTRUM, FROM the far left to the hardest right, America can agree on at least one thing: Joe Biden is a talker. In one legendary bout of talking, after a forty-minute speech at the University of Rochester, then-Senator Biden took questions for half an hour. Then an hour. A staffer held up a watch as a signal: *Time to go.* Biden ignored the signal. Two hours. Eventually his staff, exasperated, switched off the microphones so the students couldn't ask any more questions, but even that couldn't stop Joe. He just mingled into the crowd so he could keep the conversation rolling . . . then chatted for another hour.

Yet Biden wasn't always a motormouth. Just as Bruce Wayne had a childhood fear of bats, young Joey Biden was scared of talking. He had a speech impediment. A stutter.

"I talked like Morse code. Dot-dot-dot-dot-dash-dash-dash-dash," he later remembered. If you asked him his name, he might reply,

"J-J-J-J-Joe Biden." Kids poked fun at him, because kids are monsters. They called him "Dash." "It was like having to stand in the corner with the dunce cap. Other kids looked at me like I was stupid. They laughed."

Joey had three ways of coping with his stutter:

1. Family
2. Guts
3. Nuns

With the Bidens, everything starts with family. They are a tight-knit clan, something Joey would quickly learn after coming into the world on November 20, 1942, the same day that American troops marched up the coast of Africa to invade the Nazis. The Biden family was Irish, Catholic, and, therefore, large. Working class. Church every Sunday.

Joe's dad, Joe Sr., made his bread by cleaning boilers, selling furniture, dusting crops, and then selling used cars. His mom, Jean, a "spunky Irish lass with a mind of her own," would comfort him when the other kids mocked his stutter, teaching him self-respect. "Remember, Joey, you're a Biden," she would tell him. "Nobody is better than you. You're not better than anybody else, but *nobody* is any better than you." He would remember these words for decades, repeating them to his colleagues, to voters, to his kids. (His mom even had an explanation for the stutter: "Joey, it's because you're so bright you can't get the thoughts out quickly enough.")

His siblings also had his back. His sister, Val, a self-described "full-fledged tomboy," would hop onto the handlebars of his bicycle, E.T.-style, and Joey would pedal her to the playgrounds of Scranton, Pennsylvania. There he'd teach her how to throw a baseball, how to tackle, and how to shoot hoops. (Val would later return the favor. She managed every one of his campaigns until 2008.) Brothers Jimmy and Frank rounded out the Biden kids, and the foursome stuck together.

Joey had an uncle, Boo-Boo, who also stuttered, and offered him some much-needed empathy.

Yet empathy was scarce in grade school. When he read aloud his homework, one little jerk would taunt, "B-b-b-b-b-b-BIDEN!" So Joey turned to his second technique for coping with the stutter: proving that he had guts.

Joey Biden was a skinny kid. Short for his age. Yet to prove that he had mettle, he would do . . . well, basically, he would do stupid things. (In other words: boyhood.) Take the "Feat of the Dump Truck." One day, a kid named Jimmy Kennedy dared him to run under a dump truck. Normally this wouldn't be a big deal. But Jimmy dared him—or maybe triple-dog-dared him—to run under the truck *while the truck was moving.*

Jimmy was an older kid, around twelve, and should have known better. "Thing was, Kennedy never, *never*—NO CHANCE—thought the kid would *do* it . . . but Joey did it," writes Richard Ben Cramer in *What It Takes.* "The dump truck was loaded to the gills and backing up—not too fast—and Joey was small, only eight or nine, and he ran under the truck from the side, between the front and back wheels . . . then let the front axle pass over him. If it *touched* him, he was finished—marmalade—but Joey was quick. The front wheels missed him clean."

Daredevil Joey would perform more stunts. He once climbed above a construction site, grabbed a rope, and then swung over the site like he was Tarzan. On a $5 dare, he scampered up a 200-foot pyramid of coal. (That very $5 bill could later be seen, framed, hanging in his Senate office.) "Joe was just a daring guy who wasn't frightened by anything," a childhood friend remembered. Always a prankster, he tossed water balloons at rich guys in convertibles, threw snowballs into the open windows of truck drivers, and ran away from adults who chased him with a broom. (Those 2016 prankster memes? Not without basis.)

He quickly learned that football was another way to prove he had guts. When still a young and skinny kid, he found a dirt alley where some older boys were tossing around a football. "You ca-ca-can't catch me!" he said, and then ran. They tried to catch him; they couldn't. So they invited him to play tackle football, where he would play until he bled . . . and then keep playing.

Then, in 1953, in a quiet move that would send shock waves to the U.S. Senate for decades to come, the Biden family moved from Scranton to the hardscrabble neighborhoods of Delaware. (First to a town named Claymont, then to Wilmington.) Joey was ten at the time. Why the move? Money was tight, and Joe Sr. had found a better job as a car salesman. (Not coincidentally, Biden would have a lifelong infatuation with cars. He is likely the only vice president in American history whose iPhone received push-alert notifications from *Car and Driver*.)

Joe Sr.'s new job taught the kid some lessons. One year, the owner of his father's dealership, seemingly drunk with power at the annual Christmas party, took a bucket of silver dollars and emptied it onto the floor, just to watch his underlings claw for the scraps. Joe Sr. would have none of that. "I quit, God damn it!" he said, before storming out of the party.

When his parents got home that night, Joey's mom told him, "I'm so proud of your father. He just quit." Joe Sr. didn't have a backup plan, but Bidens don't get bullied. Not by a boss, not by other kids. As Senator Biden would later say, "When I got knocked down by guys bigger than me—and this is the God's truth—[my mom] sent me back out and said, 'Bloody their nose so you can walk down the street the next day.' And that's what I did."

Yet even if Joey didn't exactly get "bullied," per se, in seventh grade he was still mocked for that lingering speech impediment. In Latin class, the kids gave him the nickname of "Joe Impedimenta." So he turned to his third technique for coping with the stutter: appealing to a higher power.

Or, more specifically, nuns.

At Catholic school, nuns were a big part of young Joey's life. After hearing all of the dash-dash-dashes in his speech, a nun suggested that instead of trying to blast out a sentence in one gushing torrent, he carve it up into its natural pauses, its rhythm, its cadence. So instead of trying to say, "I love eating ice cream cones on Amtrak," you would say, deliberately, "I love—eat-ing—ice cream-cones—on Am-trak."

This strategy helped. But there was a catch: It required him to re-hearse sentences, so he couldn't really use it on the fly. What would he do when the teacher called on him in class? How would he handle conversations with strangers? What if—even scarier—he had to talk to a girl?

So he devised a few clever hacks. Let's say, for example, that he had to talk to customers on his paper route. (*Of course* Joe Biden had a paper route.) He knew that one of his neighbors was a Yankees fan. To survive a conversation with the old man, he would read up on what had happened to the Yankees the night before and then memorize a sentence in the right cadence. "Mick-ey—Mant-le—hit a—home run." Over and over. "Mick-ey—Mant-le—hit a—home run." Joey would even wear a Yankees cap when he saw the old man, hoping to nudge the conversation to his comfort zone.

He did the same thing at school, where he noticed two things. First, students were seated in alphabetical order, *A*s in the front and *Z*s in the back. Second, when a nun asked the class to read passages aloud from a book, she always did it in the same order. *Lightbulb.* So before each class, he could count the number of paragraphs and memorize the one that he was likely to recite.

WISDOM OF JOE

Map out your attack.

One day, for example, he knew the class would read aloud a passage on Sir Walter Raleigh. Joey counted the paragraphs and figured out the section that he would need to recite: "Sir Walter Raleigh was a gentleman . . . Then the gentleman put the cloak across the puddle, so the lady could step . . ."

The night before, he followed his usual routine and blocked out the cadence, getting it down cold:

Then the gen-tle
Man put the Cloak
A-cross the Puddle.

Done. He felt good about it. The next day the nun, as expected, asked him to deliver that very passage. He nailed it.

Except he was thrown a curveball.

"Mr. Biden, what was that word?" the nun asked.

Joey panicked.

"Mr. Biden! Look at the page, and read it!" the nun demanded.

But he couldn't. The word she wanted him to repeat was "Gentleman," but now, off the script of his carefully prepared cadences, the only thing he could verbalize was "Ju-ju-ju-ju-ju-gentleman." The jig was up.

Snickers.

And not only were his classmates chuckling, but this time the *nun* cut him off and said to him, mockingly, "Mr. Bu-bu-bu-bu-Biden . . ."

You've hit rock bottom when you're getting picked on by a nun. Young Joey, ashamed and furious, walked out of the classroom without saying a word. He beelined for home.

Joey told his mom what had happened, she told him to get in the car, and they drove straight to the Catholic school and marched to the principal's office, where his mother asked to see Joey's teacher. "Did you say Bu-bu-bu-bu-Biden?" his mom asked the nun. The sister confessed that she had. So Mrs. Biden, as pious and Irish Catholic as they come, stared down the nun and said that if she ever mocked Joey's stutter again, she would "rip that bonnet off" her head.

JOE BIDEN AND ICE CREAM

"My name is Joe Biden, and I love ice cream," he once said as vice president, while visiting the headquarters of Jeni's Splendid Ice Creams in Columbus, Ohio. "You all think I'm kidding—I'm not. I eat more ice cream than three other people you'd like to be with, all at once."

These creamy cravings started at a young age. After Sunday dinners, Joey would ride his bike to the pharmacy, buy a half gallon of Breyers ice cream, and then cycle home to watch what then counted as prestige TV, *Lassie*.

His favorite flavor? Classic chocolate chip. He can polish off two cones at a time. While wearing aviators. (As a Twitter meme suggests, "Find someone who looks at you like Joe Biden looks at his second cone of ice cream.") Milk shakes are fair game, too: He once tipped $20 on a $3 chocolate milk shake in a South Carolina diner.

"He gets excited about ice cream," remembers Arun Chaudhary, the ever-present videographer. "It's like a self-fulfilling prophecy to an extent, like when someone knows you like cats and they keep buying you porcelain cats to put all over your home. So the [advance team] would bring him ice cream because it's a *thing*. But he's also genuinely excited." On one trip, President Obama asked for a soft serve, and Biden ordered two scoops of the harder ice cream. He looked directly into Chaudhary's camera and said, "I ordered hard ice cream, because I'm the hard guy." ("It was funny," says Chaudhary, "but I'm glad he said it to me and not CNN.")

And in 2017, as something of a Lifetime Achievement in Ice Cream Award, Biden had a flavor named after him at Cornell University, where the students nominated flavors and voted. The four runners-up:

Biden's Chocolate Bites

Bits n' Biden

Not Your Average Joe's Chocolate Chip

Uncle Joe's Chocolate Chip

AND THE WINNER: Big Red, White & Biden

AS A YOUNG TEENAGER, BIDEN cast a hopeful eye at a private school called Archmere, a tiny, prestigious, challenging Catholic high school.

He thought of it as "my deepest desire, my Oz." Yet Oz never comes cheap. At $300 a year, the private tuition was too high for his working class parents. So Joe Biden put himself to work, applying for a summer work-study program. Instead of goofing off with his buddies, he spent his days pulling weeds, painting fences, and using vinegar to wash the school's two hundred windows.

The school accepted him, and thanks to his gardening and window scrubbing, his parents could afford it. Only one problem: The stutter continued to haunt him. It was so serious that even though the school had a mandatory public speaking class, out of Catholic mercy, they gave him an exception and let him skip the course.

So Biden kept practicing. He memorized poems and recited them in the mirror. In a bit of foreshadowing that sounds simply too rich to be true, he even memorized the Declaration of Independence, saying it again and again, hoping to master the cadence.

We hold—these truths.
To be—self—ev-i-dent . . .

If there was a theory on how to lick the stutter, Joey would try it. "Someone said a stutter was caused by facial muscles seizing up in nervous convulsion," explains Cramer. "So Joey stood for hours in front of a mirror, reading aloud or simply talking to his own image, while he tried to relax the muscles in his face, to attain that droopy, logy, sloooow eeeease that he thought would solve his problem." He also took some inspiration from the ancient Greek orator Demosthenes, who, as legend has it, honed his craft by filling his mouth with pebbles and then shouting his words to the ocean. So Joey did the same thing, reading aloud his homework while gargling pebbles and stones.

```
═══════ WISDOM OF JOE ═══════

Steal from the greats.
```

To indulge in some quick armchair psychology, it's easy here to spot the seeds of the "Biden Doctrine," which might be something like, *Stick up for the little guy.* The little guy might be a kid getting bullied, an out-of-work autoworker, or a victim of domestic violence. This theory has at least one believer: Barack Obama. "When Joe sticks up for the little guy," Obama said, "we hear the young man standing in front of the mirror reciting Yeats or Emerson, studying the muscles in his face, determined to vanquish a debilitating stutter."

Eventually Joey would become Joe, and Joe made the high school football team. He was the second-shortest guy in his freshman class, and still all skin and bones, yet he was quick, shifty, and had good receiving instincts—he could snare whatever pass the quarterback lobbed his way. This earned him a new-and-improved nickname, "Hands."

Then he grew. He shot up a foot between his freshman and junior years, emerging as one of the team's best players. Playing as a pass-catching halfback, "Hands" led the team with ten touchdowns, delighting his fantasy football owners. In one of Biden's first press clippings, a 1960 sports section of the *Chester Delaware County Daily Times* reports, "The home team scored first in the opening period when ... halfback Joe Biden ... lugged the pigskin an additional 10 yards into pay dirt." Another game recap notes that "Biden stood out for the Archers."

The team went undefeated. In what sounds like a scene from a Disney movie, in the championship game, Biden scored the winning touchdown and they won the title. The team has stayed close. In 1985 they held a twenty-five-year reunion, and in 2010 they held a fifty-year reunion, hosted by the vice president of the United States.

As Joe's time at Archmere drew to a close, he finally began to conquer his stutter. This led to a shocking revelation. He *liked* speaking in public. Hell, he was even *good at it*. All those nights spent memorizing blocks of text, practicing the cadence, and speaking to the mirror had given him a sneaky advantage: Now he didn't need to look at the text when he gave a speech, and he could make strong eye contact, ad lib, and interact with the audience.

So he began giving little mini speeches. About the world, about politics, about life. According to biographer Jules Witcover, one of his friends, David Walsh, later said that Joe "never saw a soapbox he didn't want to get up on. He was very knowledgeable about history and politics." Joe liked to talk (and talk and talk) in the backyard of the Walshes' house, sometimes with David's parents. (As a joke, his buddies would later give him an actual soapbox.)

"Joe, what do you want to do?" David's dad asked the seventeen-year-old.

"Mr. Walsh," he said, without hesitation, "I want to be president of the United States."

====

BIDEN WOULD NEVER FULLY SHAKE the memories of that stutter. Sometimes it came back. And sometimes he spotted it in others. Take a random afternoon in 1994, when he gave a presentation to an eighth-grade class that visited him from Delaware. One of the kids raised his hand to ask a question. The kid was impossible to miss: He wore a bright orange, yellow, and blue sweater from Cross Colours, that ubiquitous brand from the mid-'90s.

The Sweater Kid was Branden Brooks, or "Skip," who'd struggled with a stutter all his life. Like Biden, he was afraid to raise his hand in class. When you have a stutter, it seems that nothing is easy. Not even ordering food at McDonald's. In Branden's experience, "You don't order exactly what you want, because you're afraid of how it comes out." Talking on the phone with girls is hard. Everything is hard.

Yet when Branden heard Senator Biden's speech, he had the guts to ask a question. *Nailed it*, he thought, pleased that he didn't stumble over his words. But Biden knew. He gently pulled Branden aside and said, "I notice that you have a stutter. I used to have one, too, but I never let it hold me back. You have something important to say, and people will wait to hear it."

On that day in Washington, frankly, those words from Biden didn't really sink in. ("I didn't think of it as a big deal at the time," he said years later. "I was thirteen. And I was like, *Okay*, then we went off and had more fun in DC.")

Then he got the letter.

A few weeks later, Branden received a handwritten note from Senator Joseph R. Biden, who must have made some inquiries about how to get in touch.

Dear Branden,

It was a pleasure meeting you yesterday. You are a fine—bright— young man with a great future ahead of you if you continue to work hard.

Remember what I told you about stuttering. You can beat it just like I did. When you do, you will be a stronger man for having won. Also remember, every time you are tempted to make fun of someone with a problem, how it feels when you are made fun of.

Treat everyone with respect and you will be respected yourself.

Your friend,
Joe Biden

There were no cameras. This was no PR move. Senator Biden stopped whatever else he was doing and took the time to ink a letter to an audience of one: thirteen-year-old Branden Brooks.

Branden took Biden's advice. He began speaking up more. "I was like, he's right, I need to put myself out there, I need to not be afraid. I need to speak my mind," he says now. In ninth grade he ran for class president . . . and won. The next year he ran for class president . . . and won. Every year in college, he ran for class president. Every year he won. Every year he gave a speech in front of the school.

Emboldened by his public speaking mojo, Branden eventually went to law school. Like Biden, he wanted to go into public service. He wanted to be a prosecutor. In 2008, he was sworn in as a prosecutor by the attorney general of Delaware, a man named Beau Biden.

And because life comes full circle, in 2015, he tweeted a photo of his swearing-in ceremony, along with a picture of that letter. He thanked the vice president: "Took your advice to heart and years later Beau swore me in as a prosecutor."

Beau Biden swearing in Branden Brooks.

And the vice president responded: "And it's still true today, my friend. Treat everyone with respect and you will be respected yourself."

Biden, of course, was just channeling the words of his mother. *Nobody is better than you. You're not better than anybody else, but* nobody *is any better than you.*

2

Hot Young Biden (1960—72)

"I probably started my first year of college a little too interested in football and meeting new girls. There were a lot of new girls to meet."

AS HE MULLED OVER WHERE to go to college, Joe thought about becoming a priest. (Can you *imagine* a Father Biden? The "Holy Finger-Guns"! The Aviators Priest!) Even though he had "dated a lot of girls" by that point, he still felt the calling of the frock. The headmaster of Archmere gently suggested that before he swore any lifelong vows of celibacy, maybe he should go to college, then decide.

So he went to the University of Delaware, dated more girls, and basically turned himself into Hot Young Biden. How hot? A '60s-era photo of college Joe, where he looks a bit like a young Channing Tatum, would later break Twitter and make Leslie Knope faint. Just a few of the breathless reactions:

"Young Joe Biden could leave me on read at 4:30 and text at 8:47 and I would reply at 8:46."

"I want to go back in time and make young Joe Biden a Valentine's Day card and put it in his locker waiting in the corner for the surprise on his face as he sees the Valentine's Day card fall from out of his locker."

"If they don't remind you of Joe Biden, don't 👏 have 👏 sex 👏 with 👏 them."

It's possible that Hot Young Biden might have been a little too hot for his own good. In the fairy-tale version of this story, Biden worked his tail off in college, hit the books, and served as a role model for the youth of America. Nope. He basically loafed about, and later confessed: "I probably started my first year of college a little too interested in football and meeting new girls. There were a lot of new girls to meet."

He was still trying to meet girls in his junior year, when he drove to Fort Lauderdale with some buddies for Spring Break. Yet he was bummed to find a mob of silly drunken college kids, all of them acting stupid. (Spring Break: unchanged since the '60s.) So a couple of friends suggested that they take a quick trip to the Bahamas; it would cost only $25 for a round-trip plane ticket.

Biden wasn't really a jet-setting Bahamas guy—he had never even been on a plane—but what the hell, why not? He blew most of his spending money on the ticket, and the friends hopped on a plane to Paradise Island, Nassau, without a hotel or a plan.

They soon met some random guys who were sharing cheap accommodations, and they agreed to let Biden and his buddies crash for around $5, which meant sleeping on the floor.

Like many tropical getaways, Nassau's most beautiful beaches are private, safely keeping the rabble at bay. Joe was part of that rabble. He goofed around with his friends on a public beach, but then he saw, in what sounds like a vision, a "luscious pink pile" called the British Colonial Hotel, separated by a chain-link fence. Through this fence he saw, well, "dozens of beautiful young college girls sunning themselves."

Please keep in mind that Joe Biden was twenty-one at the time and acted like any red-blooded twenty-one-year-old: He wanted in. Yet he wasn't a hotel guest, and he sure as hell couldn't afford a room, so how could he get past that fence? Simple. Biden and his buddies found some hotel towels that were hanging on the fence, "liberated" these towels, masqueraded as hotel guests, and walked straight in through the gate.

As Biden later described the scene in *Promises to Keep*, they had opened the gates of paradise. Instant luxury, women everywhere, like a commercial for Axe body spray. Joe and his wingman soon noticed two beautiful women chilling by the pool, a blonde and a brunette. Joe and his friend quickly huddled up to debate a key procedural point:

"I've got the blonde," said Joe.

"No, *I've* got the blonde," said his buddy.

They flipped a coin.

Biden didn't wait to see who won the toss; he beelined straight for the stunning blonde.

WISDOM OF JOE

Don't wait for the coin flip.

"Hi, I'm Joe Biden."

"Hi, Joe. I'm Neilia Hunter."

She had green eyes. An easy smile. Instantly they hit it off, and the banter came quickly as Joe learned where she was from (the Finger Lakes), where she went to college (Syracuse), and what she wanted to do (teach). They kept flirting. As Joe talked to Neilia, he could see, over her shoulder, in the water, some guy emerge from a yacht. This Yacht Man—wearing "a little white yachter's cap"—walked right toward them, and it became clear he knew Neilia.

Awkward introductions all around.

The Yacht Man asked Neilia if they were still on for that night. "I'm really sorry about tonight," Neilia said, "but Joe and I are going to dinner tonight."

Game on.

And this was Neilia. Joe did indeed take her to dinner that night, despite having only $17 to his name, and winced when the check came for $20. She slipped him two twenties—*it's okay.* Later they took in some live music. On the walk home Joe tried to jump over a chain, caught his foot, and wiped out and fell to the ground. He wasn't hurt and Neilia laughed and reassured him: "It was so dark you couldn't possibly see."

As Joe said years later, he fell "ass over tin cup in love." He knew she was "The One." For the rest of Joe's time on Paradise Island he saw her every day, pretty much blowing off his buddies. Before he left the island he told her, with the certainty of young love, "You know we're going to get married."

"I think so," she whispered. "I think so."

BIDEN AND BOOZE

What's Joe Biden's favorite beer?

a. Budweiser
b. Guinness
c. PBR

He couldn't tell you. Joe Biden has never had a beer. He has never had a drop of alcohol, not even on Spring Break. You would never guess that from *The Onion*'s Joe Biden, with its headlines like, "Biden Clenches Plastic Beer Cup in Teeth to Free Hands for Clapping." And sure, when he's gleefully finger-gunning behind Obama at the State of the Union, you'd be forgiven for thinking that he might be on his third bourbon.

The reason? As a kid, he had noticed that his uncle Boo-Boo drank too much, and he wanted to avoid the same fate. "There are enough alcoholics in my family," he said in 2008. In college Biden was always the designated driver, making him the darling of the parents. (But don't worry—he still had his fun. "Joe would do wild and crazy things," as his sister, Val, later clarified, "but he was always sober.")

Biden has the same policy with cigarettes and pot. (In college, he once stopped dating a woman because she smoked—*dealbreaker*.) "I don't use anything that could be a crutch," he told a reporter in 1970. "I use football as a crutch and motorcycle jumping and skiing—I ski like a madman. But those are crutches over which I have some control. I'm against chemical crutches."

AFTER JOE RETURNED FROM THE BAHAMAS, he raced home and told Val, "I met the girl I'm going to marry!"

Val didn't laugh this off. Impulsive? Maybe. But the whole family knew that when Joe got an idea in his head, he was serious. He mooched a turquoise convertible from his father—one of the perks when your dad is a car salesman—and on the very next weekend, he drove five hours to visit Neilia in Skaneateles, New York, staying at a nearby rooming house. He met her family in their fancy house on the lake, which he later recounted in *Promises to Keep*. (Much of what we know about Joe and Neilia's early courtship, and what happens next, comes from Biden's 2007 memoir.)

"You water-ski, don't you, Joe?" her father asked, in what sounds like a deleted scene from *Meet the Parents*.

He did not. But Biden was a natural athlete—he still had dreams of playing on the college football team (and he once dreamed of going pro)—so he made it his new mission in life to become an expert water-skier. He took some free lessons from a friend of Val's, one day spending six straight hours falling down, getting up, falling down. (For the sensible people who have never tried it, six hours is a *lot* of water-skiing.) On a more substantive note, this anecdote showcases a core Biden trait: the willingness to put in the time and practice. He makes it look easy with the toothy smile and the folksy charm, but whether it's overcoming his stutter as a teenager, studying troop movements in Iraq, mastering the details of constitutional law before a Supreme Court battle, or literally busting his ass to become proficient in water-skiing, Joe Biden puts in the work.

```
═══════════ WISDOM OF JOE ═══════════

        If you want it, hustle for it.
```

Soon Neilia met the Biden family, and as they bonded over home-made barbecue, she easily won them over. How could they not be impressed with her one-two punch at Syracuse—dean's list and the homecoming queen? Joe was so in love that he scrapped his summer plans and got a job at a gas station, so he could stay in Skaneateles and spend more time with her. He pumped gas during the day and saw Neilia at night. (It's easy to imagine Hot Young Biden at the gas station, flashing a big smile and filling 'er up while he chats your ear off, and then, when the tank is full, keeping you another five minutes even though you're late for work.)

When the summer was over, Joe knew that in his fall semester, he would not be able to see her on the weekends—he had football practice. He had impressed the coaches the previous spring, and now he had a chance to be a starter. Biden had loved football since he was that scrawny little kid in Scranton. But playing football meant not seeing Neilia.

So he ditched football.

Not only did he quit the team, but he rejiggered his fall schedule so that he had no classes on Friday—a classic senior move—which freed Thursday night for the 320-mile trip to New York. Joe didn't own a car, so, when possible, he would borrow a car from his pop's dealership. If that wasn't possible? He'd hitchhike. Then he got craftier. Joe's father was plugged in to a network of dealerships that needed cars moved from one lot to another, so Joe, who had gobs of friends, paid them five bucks each to drive a car one way and hitchhike home; since the dealership paid Joe $10 per ride, he made a cool $5 profit on each trip. That could add up to $100 per weekend, which subsidized his visits to Neilia. (Joe Biden: the original Uber.)

On those car rides, with the wind in his hair, he would let his mind wander. He thought about the future. He thought about the wedding, graduation, law school, the house he and Neilia would buy, and children. ("She wanted five, and that was okay by me.") He daydreamed about running for public office. Campaigning. Giving speeches. And he wasn't alone in his buoyant optimism; a friend of Neilia's remembers a phone call where she gushed about her new boyfriend and said, "Do you know what he's going to be? He's going to be a senator by age thirty and president of the United States!"

It's entirely possible that without Neilia, Joe Biden would never have become a lawyer, a senator, or vice president. We can thank a handwritten note. When Joe drove to visit Neilia at Syracuse, he sometimes had to kill time while she was in class, so she would leave him little notes on his parked car's windshield ('60s-era texting). One day she left him a note saying that she was running late, but since he was on campus, why not check out Syracuse Law School? He did just that: He applied, was accepted, and then enrolled.

Everything was locking into place.

===

JOE MARRIED NEILIA IN 1966, and his father gave them a surprise wedding gift. Since Joe Sr. managed a Chevy dealership, he said to Neilia, "Why don't you give me [your] car, and I'll fix [it] up for ya for the wedding." But his dad had a sneaky plan. A few days later,

Joe and Neilia swung by the dealership to pick up the refurbished car, and were shocked to find a gorgeous, shiny 1967 Corvette Stingray 4-speed. Joe's dad pointed to the beauty. "This is my wedding gift."

(Biden still owns the car. In 2016, nearly fifty years later, he took Jay Leno for a spin, boasting that he had once pushed it to 110 mph. "What were you more excited about, the wedding night or the Corvette?" Leno asked him. "The wedding night," Biden said with a chuckle.)

With the Corvette as their only possession of real value, the young couple moved into a modest house in Syracuse, at 608 Stinard Avenue, just a few blocks from a small reservoir. They were broke and ate cereal for dinner, happily, in an era that Joe would later describe as magical. Joe was in law school at the time. Neilia taught at a nearby elementary school.

They made their first addition to the family courtesy of some neighbors, whose German shepherd gave birth to some puppies. The puppies were adorable (because they were puppies), and Neilia would watch them play. So to surprise his wife, one day, Joe knocked on his neighbor's door to ask if he could buy one. How ambitious was Joe Biden in his twenties? Exhibit A: They named the puppy Senator (or "Tor," for short). They took walks with Tor around the reservoir and played football in the street with the local kids. They charmed their neighbors. In the summer, Joe and Neilia hopped into the Stingray, put down the roof, and drove the neighborhood kids to ice cream at Marble Farms.

While Biden glided into his new neighborhood with ease, he had a tougher adjustment with law school. By his own admission he was "sloppy and arrogant." He didn't really find the work hard, "just boring," and he liked to play hooky. (Kids, in this case, don't follow Joe's example. Study hard. Stay in school.)

He was so casual with his coursework, in fact, that when he wrote his legal papers, he didn't understand how to cite articles. This got him in trouble. When a classmate accused Biden of plagiarizing passages from the *Fordham Law Review,* the faculty summoned him for an explanation. "The truth was, I hadn't been to class enough to know how to do citations in a legal brief," he later confessed. He *did* cite the *Fordham Law Review* in his paper, but technically, you're supposed to cite the original source every time you use a quote. He didn't. It seemed to be an honest (but careless) mistake, and the dean exonerated him, writing that "in spite of what happened, I am of the opinion that this is a perfectly sound young man." (Soon the issue was forgotten, until it would later make a damning cameo in a presidential election. . . .)

Biden assumed that no matter what he did for the first chunk of the semester, all that really counted were the final exams. So he coasted until he had to cram. With only ten days before the finals, he still had basically done nothing. *Uh-oh.* With the clock ticking, he realized he was screwed. So he made two smart decisions:

1. He started drinking coffee for the first time.
2. He asked for Neilia's help.

And "help" is understating things; the way Biden describes it, she did practically as much work as he did. "Neilia devised the strategy," he explains in his memoir. They would divide and conquer: Joe focused on two of his classes, Contracts and Property, and Neilia cracked the books on his other two classes, Torts and Criminal Law, and converted his notes into detailed, meticulous study guides that would help him master the material. The results? Neilia's guides helped him ace Torts and Criminal Law. Joe failed one of the classes he tried to do on his own (Contracts). The good news is that he passed the other class he did solo, Property. The bad news is that this is likely because, as he put it, "The professor died and they passed everybody in the class."

```
=========== WISDOM OF JOE ===========

      Don't be too proud to ask for help.
```

Biden couldn't spend all his time cramming; law school wasn't cheap, so to make some extra cash, at various points he would work at a local brewery, spend nights as a hotel clerk, and even drive a school bus, which feels very on brand. And with Neilia's help, he did enough to squeak by and graduate from Syracuse Law School in 1968, finishing #76 in a class of 85.

Then something flipped. After the less-than-stellar showing at Syracuse, Biden seemed eager to begin "real life"—to do the things that matter. The next few years would be a blur. Biden joined a corporate law firm, quit the firm (after realizing he'd rather help people than big business), launched his own law firm, and served as a public defender, where he began a lifelong quest of "fighting for the little guy."

And then Biden forever left his youth on February 3, 1969, when Neilia gave birth to their first child, Joseph Robinette Biden III, better known as Beau. Exactly one year and one day later, she gave birth to Hunter. A daughter would soon follow: Naomi. The house filled up fast and they were cramped; at one point, little Beau had to sleep in a closet. During this time, they kept moving as Biden kept busy at work, met some local Delaware politicians, and then won a seat on the New Castle County City Council, thanks largely to Val's political savvy.

Now that Hot Young Biden had turned into Family Man Biden, the Bidens eventually settled into a larger house in Wilmington, Delaware, which he called "North Star." And now, only four years out of Syracuse Law School, the owner of "Tor" cast his eyes on a new goal, an idea that seemed absurdly far-fetched: the United States Senate.

3

The Hail Mary (1972)

*"The smart guys covering Delaware politics
didn't give me a snowman's chance in August."*

THE DEMOCRATS HAD A PROBLEM. In 1972, the world had yet to learn about a building called Watergate, Nixon was still popular, and he was about to pancake George McGovern, running up the electoral scoreboard 520 to 17. Some of the Senate races were hopeless; why even put up a fight?

Take Delaware, for example. The Republicans had an incumbent, and their man looked unbeatable. Senator Caleb Boggs was a bona fide legend; a World War II hero, for the last thirty years he had been a member of Congress (three times), governor of Delaware (two terms), and now he was a U.S. senator.

He had never lost a race.

The Democratic Party bigwigs knew they couldn't beat Caleb Boggs. So they needed someone expendable, a sacrificial lamb.

A few names were tossed around. Then came one that most people had never even heard—*How about this Joe Biden kid?* (At the time, Biden was a fresh-faced New Castle County councilman, and had been networking with the Delaware political scene.)

We can imagine the chuckles. *Joe Biden! Good one.* Joe Biden was only twenty-nine years old. *That's too young to be a senator.* (It is, literally, too young to be a senator, as Article I of the Constitution says, "No person shall be a Senator who shall not have attained to the age of thirty years.")

Ted Kaufman was in that meeting where the Democratic bigwigs floated the idea of Biden running. He remembers hearing one of them ask, "Well, who's going to be his campaign manager?"

"His sister, Valerie," someone said.

"Great ticket. They ought to reverse it!"

They had a point. Whereas Joe had sort of goofed around at college, Val was a star. "Valerie had been a top student at the University of Delaware," Kaufman said. "She'd been homecoming queen. She was an absolutely incredible person."

Val was *always* in Joe's corner, and had been ever since they'd practiced tackle football and ridden together on that bicycle. When Joe ran for county councilman, Val developed a hyperorganized system that gave them an edge: She tracked all the voters in the county, sliced and diced the neighborhoods by past voting records, and established a system of block captains. The operation, in a sense, served as a crude beta version of the vaunted '08 Obama campaign apparatus. (Biden wasn't the first to do this, of course. It can be traced as far back as Aaron Burr, who, in 1800, tallied up the blocks on a voter-by-voter basis, outmaneuvering Alexander Hamilton.)

Val called up Kaufman—*Can you help us?* He agreed to meet the Biden kid. "I'll be happy to help you, but I've got to tell you that you have no chance of winning," he told Joe. Kaufman liked what he saw, however, and joined Team Biden. He would be Biden's right-hand man for thirty-six years.

Biden knew the odds were close to impossible. As he put it, the pundits said he had a "snowman's chance in August." But what the hell? Biden was not one to turn down a challenge—just ask the kid who dared him to run beneath that moving dump truck. And the former football player inside couldn't resist trying the Hail Mary.

"I am announcing today my candidacy for the United States Senate," he said on March 20, 1972, before launching into a forty-minute speech—short for him! After the speech, he hopped in an old-timey propeller plane and flew around the state, with Beau sitting on his lap. Delawareans must have wondered . . . *Who the hell is this guy?* In one early poll, 18 percent of Delawareans had heard of Biden. Caleb Boggs? 93 percent.

He had a plan to get people to know him. And it pivoted around something very simple: coffee.

Even before he officially announced, Biden knew he had to do *something* to get on the public's radar. He couldn't afford too much advertising, so he set out to do things the old-fashioned way, sitting down with voters over a cup of coffee to discuss the issues. The first coffee session would begin at 8 a.m., usually at a neighborhood woman's house, and they would invite thirty to forty of her neighbors to join. Another session would begin just down the street at 9 a.m., also with thirty guests. Then another at 10 a.m., then 11 a.m., practically back-to-back for the entire day, sometimes until midnight. As always they did things as a family; Valerie, Neilia, and Joe's mom all pitched in, showing up with coffee and doughnuts. (Joe's mom was the "coffee chairman.") He could meet with more than three hundred people per day. They sometimes brought along Beau and Hunter, and just "carried them from house to house like footballs in wicker baskets."

It's a lesson that stuck with Joe for life. Decades later, during the 2008 election, after an eighteen-hour day he turned to one of his staffers, Herbie Ziskend, and told him, "The key to winning these things is you have to ask the people for their vote." So simple, but the advice sort of blew Ziskend's mind. In all the machinations of a modern election, it's easy to forget these basic lessons, but they're the things that Joe excels at—*Just ask for their vote.*

WISDOM OF JOE

Remember the basics.

Yet back in 1972, Biden knew coffee and charm weren't enough. He knew that at twenty-nine years old, if he wanted to be taken seriously, he needed to command the issues and study the policy. So every Sunday night, Joe and Neilia invited PhDs and Fulbright scholars to their home, fed them plates of spaghetti, and then they geeked out over the tax code, domestic policy, and foreign affairs. He knew that people would ask, *Is he just an empty smile, or does he have substance?*

He gave speeches on civil rights, health care, and the folly of the Vietnam War. (Whether you agree with Biden's policies or not, you have to give him credit for saying—for the most part—basically the same thing for fifty years. For this we can thank Joe's grandfather, Grandpop Finnegan, who told him, *Tell them what you really think, Joey. Let the chips fall where they may.*)

Immediately Kaufman saw something special. *This guy, Biden, he gets it. He doesn't just spout the Democratic talking points. He thinks. He does his own thing.* "These were issues that not a lot of elected officials had been talking about: The Democrats didn't say much about balancing the budget. No one was saying that we have to do something about the environment," remembered Kaufman. "He was for a strong criminal justice system. That was a no-no among Democrats. The Republicans were the people who were concerned about crime. But Joe Biden talked about the fact that the people who were getting hurt by crime were our people."

But these principles don't go far without campaign donations, and Biden had squat. In the early days he met with potential donors; many passed. (Why squander money on a lost cause?) In one of these meetings, a potential donor told him that he had no chance, that the experts said he had no chance and even his *dentist* said he had no chance. He just ripped into Biden.

Joe stood up and turned to leave. "Look, I don't have to take this malarkey. I don't need you or this committee. And another thing . . . I'm gonna win."

MALARKEY

"Malarkey" is the most Biden-y word in the English language. But where does it come from?

The word's origin can be traced back to the early thirteenth century, when an old Irish shoemaker, Bartley Malarkey, was accused of cheating his customers.

Wait . . . that's a bunch of malarkey. The origin is unknown. *Merriam-Webster* defines it as "insincere or foolish talk." The earliest use is thought to be in the 1920s, possibly from an Irish-American cartoon. UrbanDictionary.com defines it as "an Irish-American slang word meaning 'bullshit.' Most notably used by U.S.

Vice President Joe Biden during the 2012 Vice Presidential debate."
(Another win for Biden: his very own Urban Dictionary entry.) You
get the feeling that this is a word that Joe heard while growing up in
the Biden clan, a word that helped shape his thoughts on integrity,
plainspokenness, and what it means to be a man.

One study analyzed a century's worth of public records and
found that Biden used the word "malarkey" more than twice as
much as anyone in Congress. A few classics:

> In 2012, Biden told a group of Pennsylvania firefight-
> ers that President Obama was going to invite them to
> the White House for a beer. "He's going to call you, no
> bullshit. This is no malarkey. You come to the White
> House. I'll buy you a beer."

> In 2015, Biden said, "Mark my words, the Republican
> Party is going to try to claim credit for this [economic]
> resurgence. . . . It's a bunch of malarkey."

> In 2016, Biden said that Donald Trump "is trying to tell us
> he cares about the middle class. Give me a break. That's a
> bunch of malarkey."

FROM DAY 1 OF THE CAMPAIGN, Biden made one thing clear: *No gut-
ter politics.* No attacks on personality. This conviction would become
a career-long habit, and it's one reason he's so beloved in the Senate,
by Democrats and Republicans alike. He even took the "positive cam-

paign" to hilarious extremes. At every turn he seemed to *praise* Caleb Boggs. "I don't think [anybody] can find anything unethical about Senator Boggs," he volunteered cheerfully. "He's just a very ethical guy."

Biden's one flirtation with negativity? He said that Boggs was "a nice guy, but he's just not an innovative senator." *Burn.*

And let's say you were a Cale Boggs supporter and you happened to awkwardly bump into Joe Biden on the street. If he talked to you—and of course he would talk to you—he just might open his blazer and show you a campaign button that read I LOVE CALE. This actually happened. Biden actually wore a Boggs campaign label inside his suit jacket.

Given that mind-set, there was no way he would allow his team to run a negative ad. "We produced some radio advertising in which we just really *mildly* criticized Caleb Boggs, and after it ran for two or three days, he made us take it off the air," remembers John Marttila, a longtime advisor, who helped create the '72 ads. He laughs when he tells the story. "I think one of them was on the environment, and the tagline was something like, 'When Joe Biden sees a tree, he sees a tree,' and it was so gentle by today's standards. But Joe was always, *always* adamant about a lack of negative advertising." So they pulled the incendiary ad.

WISDOM OF JOE

Never neg.

Instead of going after Boggs, he used the Vietnam War as a wedge issue, denouncing it as a "stupid and a horrendous waste of time, money, and lives based on a flawed premise," and wondering why the United States was "spending so much energy in Southeast Asia that we had left truly vital interests unattended." (Swap out "Southeast Asia" with "Middle East," and it's easy to spot a coherent through-line from 1972 to the present.)

Yet even if he was good on the issues, the age thing was a real problem. *Who runs for the Senate at age twenty-nine?* He looked so young that when he campaigned with his father (alongside Neilia and his mom), people sometimes mistook Joe Sr. for the Senate candidate. ("Hey, I'm going to vote for your dad!" people would tell Joe. He'd fire back, "I am, too!")

Val found a solution when staring at a portrait of Henry Clay, the legendary senator. Clay was twenty-nine when appointed to the Senate in 1806. (Biden's birthday, conveniently, would fall between the election and the start of the next Senate term, so he just barely made the cut.) Suddenly Joe had an easy answer. When people told him he was too young to be a senator, now he could say with a straight face, "You know, not since Henry Clay has anybody my age joined the Senate."

At every turn he would hobnob with voters. Buying milk in the grocery store? He'd talk to voters. Traveling in a car? He'd talk to voters. When driving through town, he and Neilia had a system: She'd drive, he'd ride shotgun, and then, at red lights, he'd hop out to shake the hands of random drivers. By the time the light turned green, Joe was back in the car.

One night, the governor of Pennsylvania, who was Jewish, offered to campaign for Joe in a largely Jewish community. The campaign event was at a hotel reception hall, but the room was nearly empty. *Huh. Where is everyone?* They realized that much of the absent crowd must be at a nearby wedding. "Let's go," they said, and the boys embraced their inner Wedding Crashers and charmed the crowd. (Months later, Biden would win the Jewish vote.)

"He was the Energizer Bunny," a volunteer later told Biden's biographer, Jules Witcover. "He'd never stop. If you went to a high school football game on a Saturday morning, he was there. If you went to the Acme, he was there. If you went to the Delaware football game in the afternoon, he was there. He would go to those polka dances in the old Polish section of town. He'd shake hands. He had that smile, that grin." It's a national tragedy that we do not have video footage of twenty-nine-year-old Joe Biden at the Polish polka dances.

As Biden began to generate heat in Delaware, in DC, a man named F. Nordy Hoffman looked at the slate of 1972 Democratic hopefuls. It was Hoffman's job to get Democratic senators elected. As the head of the Democratic Senatorial Campaign Committee, he helped the party figure out how to divvy up its resources—who to fund, who to snub. Before he gave anyone a nickel, he wanted to size them up.

One day he invited Joe and his brother Jimmy, who ran the campaign's finances, to his office. Joe told Hoffman that he was going to run for the U.S. Senate.

"I knew a lot about this young man, but I wanted to find out if he had guts," Hoffman remembered years later. "So I really taunted him for the first fifteen minutes: 'What makes you think you can run?' 'Why should you be chosen?' 'We don't have all the money in the world, and I'm sure you don't have it.'"

Finally, Biden looked him in the eye and said, "I don't have to take this crap from you."

Bingo. "We are going to go for you. That's what I wanted to know," Hoffman told him.

"What?" Biden asked.

"I wanted to see if you had any guts," Hoffman said.

"That was Joe Biden. He came through with flying colors," Hoffman explained. "He was going to tell me he wouldn't take my money and the hell with me."

JOE THE LIFEGUARD

Ever since his first election, Biden has been a vocal champion of civil rights. His inspiration? The swimming pool.

In 1962, while still in college, Joe made some extra cash as a lifeguard. (With his swim trunks and summer tan, it must be said, this is peak Hot Young Biden.) A dozen lifeguards worked at the Prices Run swimming pool, but he was the only white guy. He was one of the only white people in the entire pool, which was filled with hundreds of African American swimmers.

Biden played hoops with the other lifeguards. Made friends. And for perhaps the first time, he began to see the world through a different, less privileged, set of eyes. He heard stories of segregation at movie theaters, of naked racism, of how black people endured "a dozen small cuts a day."

He got along well with the community. Well, most of the community. There was one exception. The pool did have its share of what Biden called "gangs," including a group known as the Romans. And the Romans had a kid named "Corn Pop." One day Corn Pop kept bouncing on a diving board, which was against pool policy.

As Biden later told the story in *Promises to Keep*, he yelled at Corn Pop to stop the bouncing.

Corn Pop kept bouncing.

Biden whistled again.

"Hey, Esther! Esther Williams!" Biden yelled, referring to the '50s swimmer and actress, and making one of his first Dad jokes. "Get off the board, man. You're out of here." Corn Pop left the pool.

Just one problem. The other guards, who knew better, warned him that later that day, when Biden left the pool and went to his car, Corn Pop might attack him with a straight razor. *Shit.* Biden thought about calling the police, but was then advised that if he did that, he'd never be accepted into the community. *Double shit.* So he did what any sensible nineteen-year-old would do: He wrapped his arm in a six-foot length of chain.

Biden left the pool and went to his car.

Corn Pop was waiting.

Biden held up his arm. He brandished the chain he had brought, and threatened to "wrap this chain around your head" before Corn Pop could use his razor. But then he kept talking, motormouth-Biden-style, and loud enough that the whole pool could hear him. Foreshadowing his days on the Senate floor, he launched into a mini speech about how he shouldn't have called him Esther Williams, he meant no disrespect, and he apologized, although—he quickly added—it really *is* wrong to bounce on the diving board and Corn Pop shouldn't do it again, and on and on and on . . .

It's unclear if Corn Pop was amused, befuddled, or simply fell asleep during the surprising speech, but somehow the bomb was defused. No knives, no cuts, no chain-wrapping. Corn Pop and Joe even became unlikely buddies, and now the Romans had his back.

More than fifty years later, as an old man, Joe returned to that swimming pool. Wearing a navy suit instead of swim trunks, he sat in the lifeguard chair. "I owe you all," he told the crowd. "I owe this neighborhood. I learned so, so much." And by then the pool had a new name: The Joseph R. Biden Jr. Aquatic Center.

==

As the election approached, Biden still trailed in the polls by over 30 points. How could he break through? How could he mix it up? Biden had an idea for a radio ad that was, well, a tad unconventional.

In the ad, Biden approached random people at a grocery store and said, basically, "My name is Joe Biden. I'm the Democratic candidate for the United States Senate. Do you trust me?"

The shoppers would say, "No, why should I trust you?"

It seemed as if Biden was recording his very own attack ad. His team was skeptical. "You can't put an ad on the air having people testify they don't trust you!" Marttila pleaded. But Joe stuck to his guns. He sensed that a lack of trust in the system permeated the air, and he wanted to be an antidote. He flipped the message to say, "That's what's wrong with America right now. I promise you if you elect me, you'll know exactly where I stand. You'll be able to trust me."

The ad was as shoestring as it gets. "Our radio ad was a guy on our staff with a portable tape recorder, putting the microphone in the face of our mailman," Val later told NPR.

Joe's bizarro ad was joined by a series of brochures, and even though his campaign ran on fumes, the literature was slick. "Joe Biden is making an impact on the U.S. Senate and he hasn't even been elected yet," said the front page of one brochure, and then, inside, it showed photos of Biden next to veteran senators like Scoop Jackson and Hubert Humphrey, with a goal of boosting his gravitas. It worked. "The printed material became kind of a revolution for political print, and was duplicated afterwards," says Marttila. (In 2015, lifelong pundit Chris Matthews remembered these brochures as something that he had "never seen before or since . . . He looked like he belonged there [in the Senate]; in fact, like he was already there.")

Yet as wonderful as these brochures might be, they were useless if no one read them. And Biden couldn't afford the postage. Mailing a single round of brochures cost $36,000, which would shatter their meager budget. The solution? Val created the "Biden post office," a base of *thousands* of freckled teenagers who would hand-deliver these brochures across Delaware. The kids schlepped across the state on Saturdays and Sundays, when they were off from school.

Biden was big with the kids. Even though most of them weren't old enough to vote, he visited high schools and spoke to the students. Biden had a hunch that even though the fifteen- and sixteen-year-olds couldn't cast a ballot, if they got excited enough, they could maybe convince their mom and dad to vote. You could argue that in 1972, Biden was to Delaware teenagers what Obama was to college kids in 2007—short on experience, long on hope.

Biden could feel the momentum. He was closing the gap. And best of all, Caleb Boggs hadn't really done much campaigning, as he viewed his reelection as a fait accompli.

Finally it was time for debate night. The two men went back and forth congenially and respectfully, sticking to the issues. (Unlike 2016, no one threatened to throw the other in jail.) At the very end, Boggs was asked about his thoughts on the Genocide Treaty, something of a hot-button issue at the time. It was a simple question.

Yet Boggs couldn't handle it, fumbled, and said he was "unfamiliar" with the treaty. (Today, within seconds of Boggs's goof, we would pillory him on Twitter: #UnfamiliarwiththeTreaty.)

The moderator turned the question over to Joe.

Biden had thoughts on the treaty. How could he not? All of those spaghetti dinners with the PhDs and the Rhodes Scholars had paid off, and he was surprised to see Boggs wobbling. He could pounce. He could go for the kill.

Instead he said, "I'm sorry, I don't know what that is, either."

Years later he explained that if he had pressed the point it would have been "graceless," or like "clubbing the family's favorite uncle."

WISDOM OF JOE

Know when to pull a punch.

Young Biden kept it classy, he kept meeting voters, and the polls kept tightening.

Suddenly the impossible seemed very possible. The Boggs people began to sniff trouble. They started running attack ads, such as a brochure that showed a kitchen sink with the tagline "This is the only thing that Joe Biden hasn't promised you."

Yet as Team Biden neared the finish line, they were running out of money. Now the race seemed like a true toss-up. And they needed to keep their radio ads on the air. If they lost the ads, they'd lose the election. But, with ten days to go until election day, the coffers were empty.

So Val arranged a meeting with some fat-cat investment counselors. They were ready to give.

In a private meeting, they asked Biden what he thought about lowering the capital gains rate. "I knew the answer I thought they wanted to hear," Biden remembered. "All I had to say was that I'd consider it . . . and I couldn't say it. . . . I just couldn't lie to their faces." He told them he *wasn't* for changing capital gains.

The meeting ended. On the way home, Brother Jimmy told him,

"Joe, I sure in hell hope you feel that strongly about capital gains because you just lost the election."

Biden didn't look back. Instead, he took out a second mortgage on his home. The ads stayed up.

Finally, election night.

112,844 people voted for the Republican icon Caleb Boggs.

116,006 voted for Joe Biden.

He won by just 3,162 votes, roughly 1 percent of the total—or about ten sessions of coffee. That night, Boggs called him to concede.

"You ran a good race, Joe."

Biden was overwhelmed. He held the phone in his hand, choked up, and for once, he could barely speak. "I'm sorry, Senator. I'm sorry," Biden finally let out.

The Biden team held a victory party at the Gold Ballroom of the Hotel DuPont. Kaufman still remembers the euphoria in that ballroom. "I can remember just as distinctly as if it just happened. I thought to myself, 'I will never, ever believe anything is impossible again.' . . . I've seen a lot of campaigns, I've been in a lot of campaigns, and I have heard about a lot of campaigns, but to this day the greatest upset was that race."

Once he collected himself, Biden moved to address his supporters. "I hope I don't let you all down," he told them. "I may go down and be the lousiest senator in the world. I may be the best."

Two days after the election, both men, in a show of bipartisanship, were scheduled to take part in a Delaware tradition in which the winning candidate and the losing candidate race each other in go-karts, then literally bury a hatchet in the sand. (I had to fact-check this five times before believing it to be true. It's called Return Day. The day after losing an election, could you imagine John McCain, Mitt Romney, or Hillary Clinton putting on a big smile and then hopping in a go-kart?) Out of respect for his decades of service, Biden offered to let Boggs skip the race. Boggs insisted.

And that was that. Joe Biden had just become the youngest senator-elect in a century, and the second youngest in the history of the United States, and along the way, he had toppled a Delaware legend. With his wife, Neilia, and three beautiful children, he had to think of himself as the luckiest guy on the planet.

===

A FEW WEEKS AFTER ELECTION NIGHT, on November 20, 1972, Joe Biden turned thirty years old, making him eligible for the United States Senate, which would begin its session in January. In just over a month, he would take his Oath of Office. In that time he had work to do. He needed to find a new home in DC for Neilia and the kids, shop for Christmas presents and a Christmas tree, learn his way around the DC Senate offices, and hire a staff. Thanks to his popularity with the youth of Delaware, Biden had to weed through 2,500 staffer applications, and all of this by hand.

For his thirtieth birthday, he had a party at Panini Grill. The whole family gathered around a birthday cake. Wearing a crisp suit, Biden cut into the cake as three-year-old Beau and two-year-old Hunter looked on, transfixed, while Neilia, smiling, leaned over to poke the frosting.

In the coming weeks, Joe and Neilia would divide and conquer their bottomless to-do list. They both traveled to DC to hunt for a house. They found a school for the boys. It wasn't lost on Biden that he was just thirty years old and lived a charmed life, and that this moment, this time with Neilia and their children, "exceeded all my romantic youthful imaginings."

On Monday morning, December 18, 1972, Biden headed back to DC for more transition work, joined by Val, as always, who continued to serve as a confidante. Neilia stayed in Wilmington, wanting to knock out some Christmas shopping and buy a Christmas tree. She loaded up the station wagon for the errand, strapping in Hunter, Beau, and baby Naomi.

Joe was interviewing candidates for his staff. The phone rang. The call was for Val.

Biden watched his sister take the call. He saw her face go white, and somehow, through some sixth sense, he just knew.

"There's been a slight accident," Val said. "Nothing to be worried about. But we ought to go home."

Biden knew better. He just knew. He felt it in his gut. "She's dead, isn't she?"

Silence. Joe and Val, brother and sister, raced to a plane and flew to Wilmington. They hurried to the hospital. He soon learned that, as promised, Neilia had gone shopping for the Christmas tree along with the kids. On the way home, she came to an intersection, stopped at the stop sign, and then eased the car forward. A tractor-trailer rolled down a hill. She was broadsided.

Neilia and the baby had died. It was not clear if the boys would live. Hunter's skull was fractured, and the doctors feared brain damage. The crash had broken nearly every bone in Beau's body, forcing the three-year-old to remain in a full body cast.

Biden could barely speak. He just stayed with his two young boys in their hospital room, waiting, watching, praying, hoping, grieving, loving. He went numb. The days bled into each other. Dark thoughts, suicidal thoughts, began to ooze into his head. "For the first time in my life, I understood how someone could consciously decide to commit suicide," he later said. "Not because they were deranged, not because they were nuts, but because they had been to the top of the mountain and they just knew in their heart they'd never get there again."

A few days after the accident, a grief-ravaged Biden somehow managed to speak at Neilia's funeral. "The night before [Neilia] died, she was writing Christmas cards," he told the crowd. "We were both in the living room in front of the fire and I was sitting in my lounge chair, a pompous young senator thinking about the big things I was going to do in Washington." He spoke of a premonition. "We had decided not to have a fourth child because of a fear that something would happen to it. . . . We had three beautiful children. Now I have two."

Christmas came and went, and the boys stayed in the hospital. Biden felt loss, despair, and then anger. He was mad at the world. He was mad at God. "No words, no prayer, no sermon gave me ease. I felt God had played a horrible trick on me," he later wrote. In some of the rare moments when he wasn't with the boys, he would "bust out of the hospital and go walking the nearby streets. [My brother] would go with me, and I'd steer him wordlessly down into the darkest and seediest neighborhoods I could find. I liked to go at night when I thought there was a better chance of finding a fight. I was always looking for a fight. I had not known I was capable of such rage." Yet grief is a complicated thing, as is faith. In all this confusion, at one point he considered quitting politics and joining the priesthood, even reaching out to the local Catholic bishop to see if it was possible. (The bishop told him, "Look, Joe, why don't you take a year to think about this?")

He did take some time. And soon he returned from the rage and banished those thoughts of suicide. At least two things kept him alive: Beau and Hunter. He knew that his boys needed him. They had already lost a sister and their mother; no way in hell would he let them lose their father. He would keep going. He would get through this. He had to. For the boys.

That hospital room, with Beau in a body cast and Hunter nursing a crushed skull, became Joe's entire universe. Early on, when Beau had to be transferred via ambulance to Delaware Division hospital, Joe reassured the boy, "I'm going to jump right in there with you, son." The idea of "the Senate" became some abstract, distant concept that felt like another lifetime. The Senate felt suddenly small, irrelevant.

"One of my earliest memories was being in that hospital, Dad always at our side," Beau remembered as an adult. "We, not the Senate, were all he cared about."

Joe had many friends, and his neighbors rallied to show their support and condolences and love. Consumed by grief, he wasn't much interested in talking on the phone. Jimmy, his brother, would screen the calls to give him privacy. But one call came through that Jimmy had to have him take.

Biden picked up the phone. "Hello, Mr. President, how are you?"

NIXON: "Senator, I know this is a very tragic day for you, but I wanted you to know that all of us here at the White House were thinking about you and praying for you, and also for your two children."

BIDEN: "I appreciate that very much."

NIXON: "I understand you were on the Hill at the time, and your wife was just driving by herself."

BIDEN: "Yes, that's right."

NIXON: "But in any event, looking at it as you must in terms of the future, because you have the great fortune of being young. I remember I was two years older than you when I went into the House. [Laughs.] But the main point is you can remember that she was there when you won a great victory. You enjoyed it together, and now, I'm sure, she'll be watching you from now on. Good luck to you."

BIDEN: "Thank you very much, Mr. President."

NIXON: "Okay."

BIDEN: "Thank you for your call. I appreciate it."

The call was recorded and later released to the public, along with a cache of Nixon's tapes. Biden's voice is raw, spent, and wrenching. His grief was unimaginable.

How did Biden come back from this? How did he find the will to not only survive but also eventually regain the glimmer in his eye, the spark of wonder, the joy of seeing Cub Scouts on an airport tarmac? To get a glimpse into how he recovered, we can look at a speech he gave, years later, as vice president, to the families of soldiers who had died in the line of duty. To empathize with the widows and widowers and parents of slain children, he shared his own pain.

"There will come a day, I promise you . . . when the thought of your son or daughter or your husband or wife brings a smile to your lips before it brings a tear to your eye." He paused, looked at the crowd, and it was clear that he fully understood their grief. "It will happen. My prayer for you is that day will come sooner or later. But the only thing I have more experience than you in is this: I'm telling you it will come."

WISDOM OF JOE

The smile will come.

The tragedy of the accident, in a sense, helps us understand one of Biden's most fundamental qualities: empathy. He connects with people. And as he told the class of 2017 at Colby College, forming personal connections—through empathy—is the one successful trait that he sees in all the best world leaders.

> Caring about your colleague as they're dealing with a sick parent, or their child [who] graduated from college, or the child was in an accident. That's the stuff that fosters real relationships, breeds trust, allows you to get things done in a complex world. The person on the other side of the negotiating table, the other side of the political debate; a person who doesn't look like you, who lives in a community you've never visited, a person who has a different background or religion than yours. They're not some flattened version of humanity, reducible to a collection of parts and attributes. They're a whole person, flawed, struggling to make it in the world just like you.

Back in that hospital room in the winter of 1972, as he watched and prayed for Hunter and Beau, reps from the Senate were relentless in asking him to serve. Biden said no. They kept coming back. Biden said no again. The Senate majority leader, Mike Mansfield, called the hospital every day. Ultimately, Mansfield knew just what card to play: *Do it for Neilia. She wanted this. She helped you get elected. She helped you toss that crazy Hail Mary.*

Biden finally agreed, but only on two conditions.

The first was this: six months.

Mansfield kept saying, "Just give me six months, and if you don't feel that you're up for it, you can quit."

The second condition: Joe insisted that if he was going to join the

Senate, he still needed to be a father to his boys. He needed to see them every day. So unlike virtually every other senator, every day, he would commute back home to see his sons. He would make the boys his number one priority.

And he would commute by Amtrak.

BIDEN AND FAITH

After the tragedy of Neilia and Naomi, Biden's faith was tested; he was angry, and he blamed God. Yet eventually he would find peace. "Quite frankly, I just got tired of wallowing in grief," he wrote in *Promises to Keep*. "What was more self-indulgent than to think God had been busying himself with my particular circumstances?"

Many years later, after yet another life-and-death trial, Biden's dad, Joe Sr., sent him a cartoon from *Hägar the Horrible*—to give him some perspective. "I still have it on my desk," Biden said in 2011. "Hägar is in his Viking boat with his horn helmet, rowing away when a bolt of lightning comes out of the sky. Hägar gets charred. He looks up at heaven and says, 'Why me, God?!' And God comes back with 'Why not?'"

He once told a crowd, "I find great solace in my faith. I happen to be a Roman Catholic, a practicing Catholic. . . . I found that, for me, the externalities of my faith bring me a sense of peace." (Or in a slightly less serene moment, he said in 2005, "the next Republican that tells me I'm not religious, I'm going to shove my rosary down their throat.")

His son Beau once wore a set of rosaries. Joe now wears that

> very set of rosaries, always, every day, and says, "I will wear it till I die."

WHEN A FRESHMAN SENATOR TAKES the Oath of Office, typically, he or she does this in the chambers of the Senate. That wouldn't work for Biden. A few weeks after the accident, he still spent most of his days and nights in the hospital, keeping a nervous eye on Beau and Hunter.

So on January 5, 1973, Joe Biden took the Oath of Office in the chapel of the Wilmington Medical Center. The tiny room was packed with Joe's family, Neilia's parents, and even a horde of cameras and press; the tragedy had put him on the national map. Just a few feet from his father's side, little Beau Biden, three years old, wearing a sweater under a blazer, rested on a hospital bed with his leg still hoisted up in a cast.

Biden swore the oath and then said a few words. "I hope that I can be a good senator for you all. I make this one promise: If in six months or so there's a conflict between my being a good father and being a good senator, which I hope will not occur . . . I promise you that I will contact [the governor] and tell him we can always get another senator, but they can't get another father."

Soon Beau and Hunter were discharged from the hospital. *They would be okay, thank God.* Val moved into the house to help look after the boys. In the morning, Joe ate breakfast with Beau and Hunter, hustled to the Wilmington Amtrak station to catch the express, and then he came back, every night, to tuck in the boys. And before he said good night, he led them in their nightly prayers, which were inspired by his Grandpop Finnegan: They would say three Hail Marys.

PART II

MR. BIDE MR. BORK

THE SENATOR

4

Biden Time (1972—88)

"I ain't changing my brand. I know what I believe.
I'm confident in what I know. And I'm gonna say it.
And if folks like it, wonderful. If they don't like it, I understand."

As a rookie senator, in the very beginning, every day Biden kept one eye on the clock, just waiting for that moment when he could bolt for the door and head home to see Beau and Hunter. (He lucked out and had one of the desks closest to the door, so he could make a speedy get-away.) This habit came with a cost. He didn't make too many friends in the early days, and by his own admission, he "did what was necessary and no more." He focused on just one day, then the next, then the next.

Some days he wore Neilia's high school ring on his finger. He would stay bunkered in his office, alone, speaking only to his boys on the telephone. He even had a rule for Beau and Hunter: He told them that they were free to call him any time, for any reason, and no matter what he was doing, he would take the call. He could be drafting a law. He could be meeting with the secretary of state. He would always pick up.

=== **WISDOM OF JOE** ===

Always take the family calls.

He also gave the boys a "wild card," telling them that if they wanted to come with him to Washington for the day, for any reason, at any time, all they had to do was look at him and say "wild card." No questions asked. "We have an expression in our family," Biden later said. "If you have to ask for help, it's too late. We're there for each other."

He was doing right by his family, but aides from around the Senate began to whisper: *Biden wouldn't last long.*

===

BIDEN ALSO HAD A MORE quotidian problem: He still looked too young to be a senator. And no one knew who he was. Security guards would stop him in the hallways and say, "Senators only, young fella."

Take, for an example, an early meeting with Secretary of State Henry Kissinger. The meeting was in room S-116 of the Capitol building. Like a college freshman looking for his classroom, Biden jogged up and down the halls in desperate search of the room. *Where the hell is room S-116?* As Biden later shared in his memoir, he was running late, panicked, drenched in sweat. He finally found the room and stumbled through the door, Chevy Chase–style. The door crashed into a file cabinet. "Um, I'm sorry I'm late," Biden awkwardly blurted out. He looked around the table and found it packed with Kissinger and senior senators who stared at him.

Kissinger thought he was a young staffer, and then mispronounced his name as "Bid-den."

Biden didn't miss a beat. "No problem, Secretary Dulles."

It had been over thirteen years since Secretary of State John Foster Dulles stepped inside Ike's Oval Office, and it might not have been the best of jokes . . . but it was a start. The sense of humor was coming back.

Joe Biden was coming back.

He was helped along by a new buddy of his, Ted Kennedy, who showed him the ropes and took him under his wing. One day he offered to take Biden to the Senate gym, where he was introduced to three old senators . . . who happened to be buck naked. (In one of the few times of his life, Joe Biden was speechless.)

Yet the recovery from grief is not linear, and sometimes the old anger would bubble to the surface. Early in his Senate tenure, he traveled to New Orleans with his brother Jimmy to give a speech at Tulane. One night they ran into a bunch of drunken jerks. "We were walking the street late at night talking about Neilia and looking for a place to eat," he told a reporter in 1974.

These four guys were coming toward us, taking up the whole street, looking for trouble, and for a split second it flashed through my mind, "Take 'em on." We banged into each other. Nothing had happened, nothing had been said, but, you know, we were ready. I'm no fighter, and I'd probably have gotten the stuffing kicked out of me.

At that moment, a New Orleans policeman walked around the corner, and as soon as I saw him, it clicked: What the hell am I doing? I'm a United States senator letting my emotions get to the point that I'm willing to take on four toughs on a side street in New Orleans just to let the frustration out.

Back in DC, with his mind focused on work, it did not take long for

Biden to begin speaking his mind—a little too freely, for some. The Joe Biden we know and love was about to make his public debut.

In 1974, the Senate mulled over a pay hike for its members. This is an awkward topic for obvious reasons. And it's not a topic that's usually embraced by rookie senators. The economy was in the toilet, and it's never a good look to raise your salary when the middle class is out of work.

Senators were paid $42,000 at the time. Most were independently wealthy, and almost all of them needed to maintain two households, one in their home state and one in DC. Biden had no real money. He didn't own a single share of stock. He wasn't necessarily *for* the pay raise—he agreed that the timing didn't make sense—but he brazenly gave a speech supporting it to all of his senior colleagues: "It seems to me that we should flat-out tell the American people we are worth our salt. The American people would understand because they are a lot smarter than we give them credit for." Here we can imagine the stunned silence. He continued: "I do not think many of the visitors sitting up there in the public gallery or outside the Capitol feel that they want people in the U.S. Senate who are not worthy of a high salary."

You can guess the reaction, and you'd be right. One newspaper ran the headline: I'M WORTH MORE MONEY, $42,000 NOT ENOUGH. Another front-page editorial said, "The voters of Delaware who elected this stupid, conceited jackass to the Senate should kick him in the rear to knock some sense into him, and then kick themselves [for] voting [for] such an idiot." (Biden had the paper framed.)

To the chagrin of his more tenured colleagues, he spoke up in favor of public financing, arguing that it would help strip away the influence of lobbyists and outside cash—and help them win back the public's trust. His proposal: Incumbents get x dollars of public money to use for campaigning, and then the challengers get x plus 10 percent. Why the extra cash for challengers? Biden wanted to level the playing field, given the "obvious advantages of incumbency."

Only one little problem: Most of the senators relied on that outside money. And what senator wanted to give a challenger an "extra 10 percent"? Blasphemy! Biden's proposal was dead on arrival. When he finished his speech, the Senate floor was filled with more awkward silence, and later, in private, a veteran senator warned him that he would be "the youngest *one-term* senator in the history of America."

To avoid that fate, Biden would need to learn some lessons about how to treat his colleagues. Even the Republicans. One day he happened to walk past another rookie senator, Republican Jesse Helms, who, at the time, didn't exactly boast the most progressive stance on civil rights. (Helms once wrote, "Crime rates and irresponsibility among Negroes are facts of life which must be faced.") Biden, who ran on civil rights, couldn't stomach that nonsense. And he overheard Helms bad-mouthing what would become the Americans with Disabilities Act.

Biden was steamed. "That guy, Helms, he has no social redeeming value," he vented to Mike Mansfield, the Senate majority leader. "He doesn't care. He doesn't care about people in need. He has a disregard for the disabled."

Mansfield then told Joe a little story. A few years earlier, Jesse Helms—the man who "doesn't care"—had flipped through the newspaper with his wife, and noticed an ad of a disabled fourteen-year-old, who had braces on both legs. The ad said, "All I want is someone to love me and adopt me." So Jesse Helms adopted the kid.

"I felt like a fool," Biden said many years later. Mansfield gave him a piece of advice that would stick in his craw: *Joe, question another man's judgment, but never question his motives.* Why? Because you simply *don't know* his motives. Biden would think of this as the "Mansfield Method," and he mastered it.

WISDOM OF JOE

Question their judgment, not their motives.

From that moment, he vowed to "look past the caricatures of my colleagues and try to see the whole person." As he would later say when vice president, "Every time there's a crisis in the Congress . . . I get sent to the Hill to deal with it. It's because every one of those men and women up there—whether they like me or not—know that I don't judge them for what I think they're thinking."

BIDEN AND THE CAPACITY FOR CHANGE

Biden would soon meet a man who, similar to Jesse Helms, on the surface, seemed to embody everything that he opposed: Senator Strom Thurmond, the segregationist.

"Segregation in the South is honest, open, and aboveboard," Thurmond once said. To try to block the Civil Rights Act—the *Civil Rights Act!*—he gave a filibuster that lasted for a staggering twenty-four hours and eighteen minutes, an impressive feat of windbaggery, even by Joe Biden's standards. In 1965, ol' Strom was so disgusted by this "civil rights" thing that he actually *switched parties,* flipping from Democratic to Republican.

And yet.

Despite those repugnant positions, Biden did his best not to vilify the man, and he watched as Thurmond's positions on race gradually evolved. "Strom Thurmond was . . . a brave man, who in the end made his choice and moved to the good side," Biden said, more than three decades later. "I disagreed deeply with Strom on the issue of civil rights and on many other issues, but I watched him change. We became good friends."

What accounts for that shift? And how the hell could *Biden*, who had always championed civil rights, become buddies with such a . . . well, a bigot? "I went to the Senate emboldened, angered, and outraged, at age twenty-nine, about the treatment of African Americans in this country, what everything that for a period in his life Strom had represented. But then I met the man . . . I grew to know him. I looked into his heart and I saw a man, a whole man. I tried to understand him. I learned from him. And I watched him change oh so suddenly."

Biden believes in our ability to change so much, in fact, that he unwittingly used the word five times in one paragraph. "Strom knew America was changing, and that there was a lot he didn't understand about that change. Much of that change challenged many of his long-held views. But he also saw his beloved South Carolina and the people of South Carolina changing as well, and he knew the time had come to change himself."

Before Strom Thurmond died, he made sure he included one last detail in his will: The eulogy would need to be delivered by Joe Biden.

As Beau and Hunter regained their health and their spirits, Biden became more active, joined committees, and started meeting new friends and being more social. He spoke out against Nixon, making him one of the very few politicians whose longevity has permitted denouncing both President Nixon and President Trump. (This makes Biden the modern-day equivalent of John Quincy Adams, who knew both George Washington and then, at the end of his long life, Abraham Lincoln.)

And as early as 1974, Biden tipped his hand that he might be interested in running for president. "I'd be a damn liar if I said that I wouldn't be interested in five, ten, or twenty years if the opportunity were offered," he told the press at the time. "You're being a phony to say you're not interested in being president if you really want to change things. But I'm certainly not qualified at this point. I don't have the experience or background."

Yet for all Biden's emerging influence in DC, he kept himself anchored at home. "I want to make sure the people of Delaware realize that my first priority is Delaware," he said. "I feel the important thing is for me not to change from the way I was before I was elected. . . . If you hang around Washington, it's easy to start thinking you're important, so it is a blessing in disguise that I commute every day and get out of this city."

The mind-set would serve Biden well for decades. He never took the state for granted, he met with voters again and again, and amazingly, in one survey, one out of four Delawareans said that they had personally met Joe Biden. (Many have political stickers that they slap on their cars, which simply say "Joe.") Some tell stories that almost elevate Joe to folk-hero status. "Take Mary Hartnett, 72, of Wilmington," reported *USA Today*'s Maureen Milford. "She was walking home from church in 1977 when a purse-snatcher struck. Biden, who was driving by, jumped out of his car and hot-footed it after the culprit, she says, running through backyards and scaling fences. The thief dropped the pocketbook."

From purse-rescuing to schmoozing with local officials, Delaware would come first. As his foreign policy advisor Mike Haltzel remembers, Biden once told him, "If it's ever a choice in scheduling a meeting between a foreign prime minister or the fire chief from Delaware, the fire chief gets the appointment." He would never be seriously challenged for reelection.

WISDOM OF JOE

Dance with the one who brought you.

IN THE SPRING OF 1975, while strolling through Wilmington Airport, Biden couldn't help but notice some posters advertising the New Castle County park system. Now, normally, Joe Biden might or might not notice a random poster about trees. (Although as that '72 ad reminds us, "When Joe Biden sees a tree, he sees a tree.")

Yet this poster had something else going for it: a beautiful woman. "She was blonde and gorgeous," Biden later remembered. "I couldn't imagine who was looking at trees with her in the photograph." He thought, *That's the kind of woman I'd like to meet.*

Call it serendipity, call it chance, call it fate. According to at least one version of this story, that very night, his brother tried to set him up on a date and slipped Biden a woman's number. "You'll like her, Joe," he assured him. "She doesn't like politics."

Her name was Jill. As he tells the story in *Promises to Keep*, Joe called her the next day. "Um, this is Joe Biden?" he said in a strong opening. They exchanged just a bit of small talk, and he blurted, "Do you think you could go out tonight?"

"No," she said. "I have a date."

But a trivial matter like that was not going to stop Joe Biden. (*Don't wait for the coin flip.*)

"I'm only in town for one day, see," he said. "Do you think you could break it?"

It turns out she was free after all. He later drove to her place and knocked on her door like a gentleman (as opposed to just meeting at a bar), and he wore a suit, which impressed her. When the door swung open, he was astonished to see the woman from the park ads.

They went out for dinner and a movie; Jill doesn't remember the film, but their choices would have likely included *The Stepford Wives*, *Funny Lady*, and *At Long Last Love*. They stayed out till midnight.

And in something of a he said/she said, Jill remembers the story just a bit differently. Decades later, she said that Joe saw the poster and told his brother Frank, "Oh, that's the kind of girl I'd like to date!" Frank happened to know Jill from college, so he asked for her number and slipped it to Joe. (Either way, it's a solid meet-cute.)

"I was really charmed by him," she said in 2012. "At the door, you know how guys are usually trying to 'make their moves'? He didn't. He was a gentleman." After she said good-bye, at 1 a.m. she phoned her mom and said, "My God, I think I finally met a gentleman."

WISDOM OF JOE

Don't "make a move." Be a gentleman.

He asked to see her again. She agreed. More phone calls, more dates, more lovable-Joe loquaciousness. Biden was so enchanted, he tried to have a DTR (Define the Relationship) talk after *two dates(!)*, suggesting that they stop seeing other people. Jill wasn't yet ready. When she was still in college, she had married very young, and, while separated from her husband, she was still in the process of getting a divorce. And she also really, really, *really* didn't want to date a politician.

So how did Joe handle this? Whether he knew it or not, he executed the only move you can when the other person says, "I don't want anything serious": You basically agree—*let's just have fun!*—and secretly hope that the other person will change their mind.

Joe fell hard. He fell for her character, her spunk, her streak of independence. "She had backbone. She was private—Joe liked that, her cool way of hiding the girl inside, and old hurts ... he could see that," suggests biographer Richard Ben Cramer. "She had that way of looking at you ... and then that quick shy smile, half-doubting—she could sniff out bullshit. She'd tell him, too—especially when it was his bullshit—she'd tell him straight. Very soft of manner was Jill, but smart: she knew who she liked."

As the days and weeks ticked by, the fun turned into something more. Jill met his sons. They liked her. Soon Biden met Jill's extended family, won over her grandparents, and was delighted to learn that they cooked spaghetti on Christmas Eve, just like his family. When he thought about buying a new house, he took her with him to see it. (*Hint, hint.*) They spent Christmas together. In other words, this *totally-nothing-serious couple* behaved exactly like a couple that wanted to get serious.

Even Hunter and Beau knew what was up. And they approved. In a delightful anecdote shared by Biden in *Promises to Keep*, one morning, while Joe was in the bathroom shaving, the two boys approached him nervously.

"You tell him, Hunt," said Beau, then seven years old.

"No. *You* tell him," said Hunter, then six.

"Beau thinks we should get married," said Hunter.

Joe looked at them. "What do you mean, guys? Beau?"

"Well, we think we should marry Jill," Beau said. "What do you think, Dad?"

Joe liked the idea. Hunter liked the idea. Beau liked the idea. There was only one person who didn't like the idea: Jill. Biden proposed to her, and she said no. (Thank God this wasn't on the jumbotron.) She loved Joe but she wasn't ready to be a full-time mom, and like any sensible person, she still didn't want to date a politician.

So he asked her again; again she said no.

He asked her a third time.

Again she said no.

Maybe . . . fourth time's the charm?

Nope. Again she said no—still needed more time.

Okay, how about the FIFTH MARRIAGE PROPOSAL?

Thanks, but no thanks.

Finally Biden could take no more. "I'm not going to wait any longer," he told her, before leaving on a ten-day senatorial trip to South Africa. "Either you decide to marry me or that's it. I'm out. I'm too much in love with you to just be friends. Think about it while I'm gone," he told her, and then he boarded a flight to Africa. For the next ten days, he waited in agony.

WISDOM OF JOE

Keep your self-respect, even when lovesick.

Joe flew back from Africa ... and found that his ultimatum had worked. She said that she couldn't afford to lose him. This time she had a different answer: *yes.*

When Joe married Jill on June 17, 1977, they did it as a family: Hunter and Beau stood at the altar. After this simple ceremony in the United Nations chapel, they took a "honeymoon" as a family, with the four of them heading to Broadway to see *Annie*, chow down on burgers at Blimpie's, and then crash at their hotel in Manhattan ... where Joe and Jill took the smaller bedroom, giving the boys the honeymoon suite.

Many years later, a reporter asked Beau about Jill, his stepmom.

Beau immediately jumped in to cut her off. "My *mom,*" he clarified.

"You don't call her your stepmom?" the reporter asked.

"I don't. I've been a lucky man in many ways. I've had two moms," Beau said, tearing up. "It was like that from the very moment we got married. . . . Anyone who knows her knows how kind she is. Look, it's easy to fall in love with my mom."

In 1981, Jill gave birth to a daughter, Ashley. Biden began to feel whole. In the next few years he would climb the ladder of seniority, draft legislation, serve on committees. In little over a decade, he had transformed himself from a broken widower into one of the shining stars of the Democratic Party, who seemed ready to level up.

He spoke up about Watergate, the Nixon resignation, civil rights, school busing. As the boys and Ashley grew older he began to travel to more countries, he met more foreign leaders, and he joined the Foreign Relations Committee, which he would eventually chair. As for the Oval Office? In 1984, he didn't run for president—he said he wasn't yet ready—but he had turned enough heads to receive one symbolic electoral vote.

But in 1988? Joe Biden was ready.

5

Biden v. Bork (1987–88)

"Judge Bork, I guarantee you this little mallet is going to assure you every single right to make your views known. . . . That is a guarantee."

IMAGINE A YOUNG POLITICIAN GIVING A SPEECH. The words are poetic, uplifting, packed with inspiration. "It's time we hear the sound of the country singing and soaring in the dawn of a new day," he says. "It's time to restore America's soul. . . . Our time has come!"

This almost sounds like JFK, Ronald Reagan, or Barack Obama, right? Yet in the mid-'80s, it was Joe Biden who was preaching Hope and Change. Nowadays we tend to think of Biden as the cool dad or the elder statesman, but once upon a time, at age forty-four, Biden seemed like the fresh new face of the Democratic Party. Good-looking. Clean. Articulate.

Would he run for president? He made it crystal clear: "I'm not going to run in 1988."

And then he ran for president. And why the hell not? The Republicans had just enjoyed two terms in the White House, and no party had won three in a row since the days of FDR—a good sign for the

Democrats, right? Biden looked around at the other presidential hopefuls: Gary Hart. Jesse Jackson. Michael Dukakis. Some rookie named Al Gore. None of them had dibs. (There were so many candidates, they were nicknamed "The Seven Dwarves.") After sixteen years in the Senate, he now had tenure, sex appeal, and hair that was still more brown than gray. Gaffes? Not yet. This was Prime Biden.

He had just two problems. First, polls showed that only two out of five Americans knew who he was. Second, many commentators claimed that he was all razzle-dazzle, but there was no "there" there. As the *Los Angeles Times* framed it, "Although no one questions Biden's ability to rouse an audience, this very gift has helped crystallize the most significant criticism ... that there is less to him than meets the eye (and the ear); that he sells the sizzle but is short on the steak; that he is more of a show horse than a workhorse." Was Biden sizzle or was he steak?

Happily, and just in time for the '88 election, Biden would have a plum opportunity—in the national spotlight—to prove that he had the right stuff: the Bork nomination, which sounds like a lost *Star Trek* film.

To quickly brush up on our '80s political history, in 1987, Ronald Reagan told the nation that his top domestic priority was to seat Robert Bork on the Supreme Court. "No man in America and few in our history have been as qualified to sit on the Supreme Court as Robert Bork," Reagan assured us.

Bork was a legal badass. Even the Left acknowledged his intellectual firepower and Justice-y credentials. Yet he was also a constitutional "originalist" and, by some accounts, the most conservative nominee the nation had ever seen. His confirmation would tip the balance of the Court. (It didn't help that Bork had been a key chess piece in President Nixon's Saturday Night Massacre; as solicitor general, Bork had fired the Watergate special prosecutor, Archibald Cox.)

The Left mobilized. Ted Kennedy charged that "Robert Bork's America is a land in which women would be forced into back-alley abortions, blacks would sit at segregated lunch counters, rogue police could break down citizens' doors and make raids, and schoolchildren could not be taught about evolution. Writers and artists would be censored at the whim of government." The executive director of the NAACP promised, "We will fight it all the way—until hell freezes over, and then we'll skate across on the ice."

The Right, of course, thought this was hogwash, and charged that liberal "special interest groups" were putting politics ahead of country. (Any of this sound familiar?)

The hearings would run through the Senate Judiciary Committee, which, in turn, would be chaired by Joseph R. Biden Jr. It didn't look like a fair fight. Pundits such as George Will predicted that Bork would be "more than a match for Biden in a confirmation process that is going to be easy."

To compare the two men's résumés:

ROBERT BORK	JOE BIDEN
Judge on the United States Court of Appeals for the DC Circuit	Chair of the Senate Judiciary Committee
Solicitor general	Briefly served as public defender
Yale law professor	In a class of 85 students, finished #76 at Syracuse Law School
Looks a bit like a young George R. R. Martin, with piercing dark eyes and an epic, bushy beard that lends itself to thoughtful stroking	Owner of a '67 Corvette Stingray, who can knock back two ice cream cones in a single sitting

Why did this confirmation matter so much? For the nation, you could make a solid case that it was the most pivotal Supreme Court nomination of the past century. And for Joe Biden, this was his on-ramp to the presidency. His team was banking on it. "We thought the Bork nomination was going to be an incredibly positive experience," remembers Ted Kaufman, Biden's right-hand man for more than three decades. "Our basic game plan went like this: Break out in Iowa, do well in New Hampshire. The Bork nomination was going to be the opportunity for Americans to see Joe Biden for the first time, to really think about him as a president." The *New York Times* even had a photo of Bork and Biden going jaw-to-jaw with the caption "The First Primary."

Enter the gaffes.

In the weeks before tip-off, Biden promised Bork that he would get a fair hearing. Yet at the same time, reporters asked if he would vote against Bork, and he admitted that was the "overwhelming prospect."

Huh. People scratched their heads and wondered how both of these statements could be true. Critics pounced. One critic of Joe Biden was Joe Biden. He soon said that he had just made "the biggest mistake of my political career in coming out against Bork the way I did."

But then that mea culpa seemed to cause even more problems, as the Left interpreted it to mean "I made a mistake in opposing Bork." So Biden then clarified his clarification, explaining that it was "more of a public-relations mistake than a substantive mistake." As biographer Jules Witcover notes, "He seemed unable simply to shut up."

To Biden, though, the situation wasn't complicated: Given what he knew of Bork's record, he was highly, highly unlikely to vote for him, but he also kept an open mind, and he thought the man deserved a fair shake. This is a reasonable and logically coherent position, but it makes for a lousy sound bite. (A classic Biden conundrum.) By neither squarely denouncing Bork nor hiding his reservations, he found a way to tick off everyone.

So Biden did his homework. He dug deep and read Bork's opinions and papers—hundreds, thousands of pages—and surrounded himself with a team of constitutional all-stars, both liberal and conservative. His team assembled a massive compendium known as "The Book of Bork," unwittingly foreshadowing this very book.

One of these legal experts was Larry Tribe, a professor at Harvard, who has argued before the Supreme Court more times than Meryl Streep has been nominated for an Oscar. Tribe remembers these working sessions well. He says that Biden pursued the details "as though he were preparing to take a comprehensive oral exam for a PhD, or to teach a seminar to a group of smart and intensely interested students."

Biden took notes. He kept going deeper, asking Tribe to describe in detail the historical origins of key constitutional doctrines, the scholarly and judicial debates about competing modes of interpretation, the lines of precedent in the Supreme Court and lower courts, and the practical consequences of agreeing or disagreeing with various opinions. (In other words, Biden didn't just get his opinion from *Fox & Friends*.)

WISDOM OF JOE

Seek the core principles.

After all this analysis, Biden decided, *Okay, we need to keep this guy off the Court.* Yet he had to do it the right way. Biden wanted to defeat Bork on the merits, not through a takedown of his character.

Despite pressure from the Left, he refused to frame Bork as a racist or a sexist. (He was even urged by some to subpoena Bork's video rental records, hoping to uncover porn. Biden spiked the request—*Never neg.*)

The logic? Biden believes that attacks on personality aren't just shady, but that they also backfire. An assault on Bork's character, sure, would toss some red meat to the Left, but it would lose the center. Biden's approach might cost him some liberal street cred, but as Grandpop Finnegan would say, *Let the chips fall where they may.* He insisted that the Democrats "didn't have the votes to stop Bork if they were going to play to the liberal base."

So what was it, exactly, that made Bork so toxic? As Biden saw it, Bork refused to acknowledge any rights that were not explicitly spelled out in the Constitution. As every schoolkid knows, the Constitution gives a shout-out to the freedoms of speech and religion. But privacy? Nowhere is the word mentioned. Whether a right to privacy can be *inferred* is one of the holy wars of constitutional scholarship, but the Court had generally upheld that right, specifically in *Griswold v. Connecticut.* (Stay with me here. *Griswold v. Connecticut* established that a married couple has the right to use birth control in the privacy of their own home, and, more important, established a fundamental "right to privacy." A handy, if not technically perfect, way to remember this: On the way to Walley World, Clark and Ellen Griswold had plenty of sexual hijinks, and the two of them got frisky in the privacy of their hotel room. *Griswold v. Connecticut* safeguarded these rights.)

As a strict originalist, Bork disagreed with the Court, which troubled Biden. A new interpretation of the right to privacy could overturn protections on abortion, voting rights, and even the right to use birth control in the privacy of your own home. However, Biden worried that this important debate could get lost in the legalese, so he wanted to frame it in simple terms that would translate to all Americans. What do people care about? What unites men and women, black and white, gay and straight, Yankees fan and Red Sox fan?

Finally he had his answer.

Sex.

===

MEANWHILE, THE BIDEN CAMPAIGN FOUND its groove. "We were doing very well," remembers Kaufman, Biden's longtime No. 2, who reported, "There were surveys in Iowa that were showing that he was breaking out."

And Biden knew it. *Felt* it. He addressed the crowds with a growing confidence, a swagger. But to understand what turned the tide for Joe Biden in 1988, we need to look across the Atlantic. In the election for prime minister, Labour Party candidate Neil Kinnock ran against the heavily favored Margaret Thatcher. Like Biden, Kinnock could give a mean speech. He talked about his coal-mining ancestors, and asked, "Why am I the first Kinnock in a thousand generations to be able to get to university? Is it because all of our predecessors were thick? Did they lack talent? Those people who could sing and play and recite and write poetry, those people who could make wonderful, beautiful things with their hands? . . . Of course not. It was because there was no platform upon which they could stand."

Biden happened to catch the speech while flicking through TV. He liked it. He liked it a lot. He especially liked the bit about how *there was no platform upon which they could stand*, as it neatly summed up the key principles of the Democratic Party. And in a happy coincidence, Kinnock's roots had echoes of Biden's own family experience, as Biden had "ancestors from the coal-mining town of Scranton."

So he began quoting Kinnock in his own stump speeches. Each time, he was careful to clearly reference Kinnock. The crowds lapped it up.

Then came the primary debates. On August 23, 1987, Biden took a flight to Des Moines for a showdown at the Iowa State Fair with Michael Dukakis, Jesse Jackson, Al Gore, and the rest of the Seven Dwarves. He needed to do well. But since he was so consumed with Bork, he hadn't spent any time on debate prep. When his plane landed in Des Moines, he copped to his advisors that he hadn't even written a closing statement. He had nothing.

"Why don't you use the [Kinnock] stuff?" someone suggested.

Good call. There was no time to scribble out a speech—he would have to wing it. So at the close of the debate, and drawing from memory, Biden just did his normal riff on Kinnock. But he rushed it. On the stump he had plenty of time to give the full Kinnock quote, and then pivot to how it applied to his life and the lives of all Americans. Yet in Iowa, as the seconds ticked by on the debate stage, he bulldozed through the passage.

"Why is it that Joe Biden is the first in his family ever to go to university? . . . Is it because our fathers and mothers were not bright? . . . It's not because they didn't work as hard . . . they didn't have a platform on which to stand."

Nailed it, he thought. The crowd was silent, enthralled, and even in tears. Biden left the stage feeling pretty good about things.

Only one problem. An aide leaned in and said, "Pssst, you forgot to credit Kinnock."

Shit. In his hurry, he had failed to squeeze in the usual accreditation. Prior to this, he had never claimed it as his own, and it had never been a problem.

In the parallel universe, on Earth 2, in the closing statement of that fateful debate, Joe Biden simply says, "Like Kinnock, I believe that . . ." He continues to gain momentum in the polls. He wins the Iowa primary—not a stretch. Propelled by Iowa, he rides the momentum to secure the Democratic nomination. (Fun fact: At one point Michael Dukakis led George H. W. Bush in the polls, but then he wilted down the stretch, thanks, in part, to that disastrous photo of him on a tank. Biden would have looked good on a tank. Biden would have looked *great* on a tank.) With his strong appeal to the middle class, Biden wins a nail-biter of an election and is sworn in to office on January 20, 1989. President Biden gives an inaugural address that lasts ninety-six minutes—the longest in history. It is praised by many, but critiqued by some for accidentally insulting ballet dancers, the city of Bismarck, and flutists.

On Earth 1, however, Biden did not insert those two words, "Like Kinnock." At first there was no fallout. A week went by. Then two. Then, nearly three weeks after the debate, the hammer fell. The *New York Times* unleashed a front-page headline: DEBATE FINALE: AN ECHO FROM ABROAD, which charged that Biden had "lifted Mr. Kinnock's closing speech with phrases, gestures, and typical Welsh syntax intact for his own closing speech . . . without crediting Mr. Kinnock." (Bonus trivia: The story was fed to the *New York Times* by a staffer of Michael Dukakis. More bonus trivia: The story was penned by an up-and-coming political reporter named Maureen Dowd.) Just one of the many damning parallels:

KINNOCK: "Did they lack talent? . . . Those people who could sing and play and recite and write poetry? . . . Why didn't they get it? Was it because they were weak? Those people who could work eight hours underground and then come up and play football?"

BIDEN: "Those same people who read poetry and wrote poetry and taught me how to sing verse? . . . Is it because they didn't work hard? My ancestors, who worked in the coal mines of Northeast Pennsylvania and would come up after twelve hours and play football for four hours?"

Biden was soon accused of *another* bout of plagiarism, suggesting a troubling pattern. Earlier in the year, he had given an inspiring address that clearly lifted language from a 1967 Robert Kennedy speech. Then it got even worse. In another speech, Biden appeared to have cribbed some lines from Hubert Humphrey. In both cases, it seems clear that Biden didn't personally know about the lifted language, as the speeches had been written by his speechwriters. But still. On news channels, TVs showed Kennedy's speech and then Biden's speech, back-to-back. It was devastating.

Not only were the reports a headache, he started having actual headaches. Migraines. As Biden began popping ten Tylenols a day, William Safire called him "Plagiarizing Joe." Others piled on. As a pundit told the *New York Times*, "This controversy plays into the case his opponents would like to make against him: that he is a person of style rather than substance."

Exasperated, he focused on the one thing that he could control: Bork.

===

FINALLY, AFTER WEEKS AND EVEN months of hype, on September 15, 1987, Biden swung the gavel to kick off the Bork proceedings.

Gavel in hand, Biden addressed the bearded nominee. "Judge Bork, I guarantee you this little mallet is going to assure you every single right to make your views known, as long as it takes, on any grounds you wish to make them. That is a guarantee, so you do have rights in this room, and I assure you they will be protected." (As the *Washington Post* quipped, "Biden did everything but rush over to Bork's water glass with an ice-cold refill.")

In his opening statement, Biden quickly moved to frame the debate on his own terms: "We must also pass judgment on whether or not your particular philosophy is an appropriate one at this time in our history. . . . As a matter of principle I continue to be deeply troubled by many of the things you have written . . . our differences are not personal." He then rattled off the bits he was troubled by: a lack of protection of voting rights, privacy in child raising, privacy in birth control.

He kept coming back to that core issue—privacy. Channeling the Founders, he continued: "I believe all Americans are born with certain inalienable rights. As a child of God, I believe my rights are not derived from the Constitution. My rights are not denied by any majority. My rights are because I exist. They were given to me and each of my fellow citizens by our creator, and they represent the essence of human dignity." This was Biden at his finest: clear, composed, even . . . concise.

Your move, Bork.

Bork then gave a careful reply that sounded very, very smart without really tipping his hand. (This has become standard procedure for Supreme Court nominees.) He said that "the judge must speak with the authority of the past and yet accommodate that past to the present." (Who could argue with that?) "That does not mean that constitutional law is static. It will evolve as judges modify doctrine to meet new circumstances and new technologies." Bork was on his game.

Biden knew that if they lobbed abstract speeches back and forth, Bork would win. He needed to cut to the core of issues that people would care about. He thought of the Delaware voters who would care about the right to use birth control in the privacy of their own home—who cared about, well, sex.

And now Biden was rewarded for his homework, as he calmly pulled out an old Bork statement. Biden read Bork's words back to him: "the right of married couples to have sexual relations without fear of unwanted children is no more worthy of constitutional protection by the courts than the right of public utilities to be free of pollution control laws." He looked up at the esteemed judge. "Am I mistaking your rationale here?"

"With due respect, Mr. Chairman, I think you are."

It was on.

The two men went back and forth, making for some riveting C-SPAN. Biden kept pushing Bork on the question of privacy. "As I hear you, you do not believe that there is a general right to privacy that is in the Constitution," Biden challenged.

"Not one derived in that fashion," Bork replied. "There may be other arguments and I do not want to pass on those." In other words, Bork thought it would be perfectly reasonable to protect a couple's right to privacy, but he couldn't locate that rationale in the Constitution.

Biden wanted to know, *Okay, so if the right is not guaranteed in the Constitution, then where do you find that protection?* Bork didn't have an answer.

The first day soon ended. The underdog Biden had won the first round, or at least battled Bork to a draw. What Bork didn't know—what no one could know—is that Biden had prepared so thoroughly, he'd even had a "mock hearing," with Harvard's Larry Tribe sitting in a fake witness chair, pretending to be Bork. "I didn't grow a Bork beard," he remembers now, "but I did nearly everything I could, short of that, to simulate what I predicted Biden would be up against." (Biden loved the role-play, telling Tribe that he'd been a "better Bork than Bork.") Biden was taking a page from his own childhood play-book, when he'd figure out which passage the teacher would make him read aloud in class.

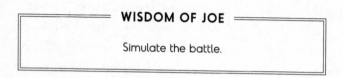

WISDOM OF JOE

Simulate the battle.

Let's take a quick time-out: This could go on for another seventeen pages—or another seventeen books—but the point is that instead of using trickery or vilifying his opponent, Biden engaged in a sober, nu-anced debate of the law. An honest, principled clash of ideas and ideals. And despite Biden's reputation as the Ray-Ban–wearing, fun-loving prankster, underneath this is a man of substance who has a command of the details.

And yet . . .

He's also a man who can make mistakes.

Back to the campaign.

———

MAYBE BIDEN COULD HAVE WIGGLED his way out of the Kinnock scan-dal. Same for the Bobby Kennedy scandal. Same for Hubert Humphrey.

But then another shoe dropped: Biden was accused of puffing up his academic record. A refresher: His class at Syracuse Law School had eighty-five students. Biden graduated in the bottom half, #76 to be exact. Without Neilia's help, who knows if he would have even passed the finals. Yet when a reporter grilled him, Biden defended his marks and said that he'd "ended up in the top half of my class." Oops.

Clearly frustrated with the never-ending questions, Biden snapped at the reporter, "I think I probably have a much higher IQ than you do, I suspect." *Oh, Joe.* The whole yucky exchange was caught on C-SPAN. He also claimed to be "the only one in my class to have an academic scholarship," but in reality, the scholarship was half merit, half need. There were other slipups—each one had an innocent(ish) explanation, but each looked damning. And those migraines continued.

Remember when Biden made that little citation blunder in law school? It came thundering back. The press pounced, spinning this as "Biden Cheated in Law School," despite Joe's insistence that he had only made a citation mistake—little more than a formatting glitch. And he had proof. Biden rummaged through his old files and found a smoking gun that could exonerate him, a letter from the dean that said: "Mr. Biden is a gentleman of high moral character. His records reflect nothing whatsoever of a derogatory nature, and there is nothing to indicate the slightest question about his integrity."

But that fifteen-year-old letter didn't fit into a sound bite. Nor did his explanation for how the Kinnock speech was usually credited, but in Iowa—just that one time—it was not. Besides, once a candidate gets slapped with a label, it's difficult to shake the image, no matter if it's fair or if it's bunk. And every time new evidence seems to fit that label, it's particularly damaging. (See also: "Crooked Hillary.")

Jill, for one, was incredulous. As long as she had known Joe, ever since that first date when he politely shook her hand when he said good night, she had known him as a man of honor. He had that saying of his—*I give you my word as a Biden.* Integrity was his bedrock. "Of all the things to attack you on," she said to him, "your integrity?"

Biden couldn't believe it either, and rebutting all of these charges must have felt something like Whac-A-Mole. Especially with the benefit of thirty years of hindsight, it really does look like each of these episodes has a solid explanation. At no point did he intend to cheat.

Yet he finally resigned himself to a more humbling truth: "It was my fault. When I stopped trying to explain to everybody and thought it through, the blame fell totally on me," he later wrote, accepting responsibility for coasting in law school, flubbing the citations, and blowing his gasket to say "Wanna compare IQs?" He owned the mistakes.

And now he had to make a decision. Stay in the race and keep whacking moles, or quit the election to focus on Bork? He still had a shot. If he set up shop in Iowa and doubled down on the campaign, maybe he could still win this thing. What was more important: the personal ambition to become president, or the fate of the Supreme Court?

There would be no flashy news conference. Biden didn't make a big stink about things, but instead, quietly, while on a lunch break from the Bork proceedings, he stepped outside to address the reporters and the cameras. Jill stood at his side.

"Hello, everybody. You know my wife, Jill," he begins. "Although it's awfully clear to me what choice I have to make, I have to tell you honestly I do it with incredible reluctance—it makes me angry," he said, in something of a *sorry-not-sorry!* "I'm angry with myself for having been put in this position. . . . I have made mistakes. . . . Now the exaggerated shadow of those mistakes has begun to obscure the essence of my candidacy and the essence of Joe Biden." That last sentence, in a sense, encapsulates the irony of Biden's career: the "shadow of mistakes" has obscured the essence—a man committed to integrity, his family, and public service.

He quickly wrapped up the speech. "And lest I say something that might be somewhat sarcastic, I should go to the Bork hearings. Thanks, folks."

```
============ WISDOM OF JOE ============

            Know when to leave.
```

Seconds later, Joe turned to head back inside the Senate building. Jill grabbed his arm and looked him in the eyes. And then she said, as Biden remembered, "something that sounded like profanity. Jill didn't often use profanity, but she wanted my full attention. She wanted me to understand that doing my best wasn't good enough now: 'You have to win this thing!'"

Cue the *Rocky* music. Biden felt galvanized. He might have lost the election, but he vowed to win the battle that, in a sense, could be more consequential to the nation: stopping Bork.

BIDEN'S PRIZE FIGHTS

When your career spans from the days of Muhammad Ali to the era of Ronda Rousey, you're going to have some one-on-one dust-ups. Some quick highlights of other Biden sparring matches:

Biden v. Jimmy Carter
The two weren't enemies, but Biden wasn't a fan of what he called his excessive "moralizing." He once told the then-president, "You thump that Bible one more time, and you're going to lose me, too."

Biden v. Fund-raising
Joe Biden doesn't like fund-raising. Never has. He *hates* outside

money and he likes to stay clear. As former staffer Jeff Connaughton tells the story in *The Payoff: Why Wall Street Always Wins*, one day Biden told his team that he was ready to hit the phones and make his fund-raising calls. "Later in the campaign, a twenty-three-year-old fund-raising staffer got into a car with Biden with a list of names and phone numbers. 'Okay, Senator, time to do some fund-raising calls.' Biden looked at him and said, 'Get the fuck out of the car.'"

Biden v. Paul Ryan

In the 2012 election, just eight days after Obama got shellacked by Mitt Romney in the first presidential debate, Team Obama, suddenly wounded, needed a strong showing from Joe. He delivered. In the VP debate, Biden's "high-energy performance—part angry bar-room debater, part condescending elder uncle, part comic mime artist—frequently seemed to leave Paul Ryan overwhelmed," judged *The Guardian*. He kept things peppy and upbeat, calling Ryan "my friend" fourteen times, but at every turn he told Ryan, "That's a bunch of malarkey."

Biden v. Donald Trump

Ah, what might have been. (Or what still might be . . .) While Biden has generally kept personality out of politics, he is, first and foremost, a father. So after Trump's "locker room talk" about grabbing women's genitalia, Biden was asked if he wished he could debate Donald Trump. "No," he replied. "I wish we were in high school and I could take him behind the gym."

Usually, when a candidate drops out of an election, they are free to go home and lick their wounds. "I'm telling you, if this had been me, I would have been curled up in the fetal position, crying," said Kaufman. "If I had undergone a barrage like that on myself and my personal integrity . . . I'm not a drinking person, but I would have seriously considered drinking."

Biden did not go fetal. He did not hit the bottle. Instead he went back to work. Tuning out the embarrassing press and the cheap shots, he called a platoon of legal witnesses to the Senate floor. He wanted to show that while Bork might be brilliant, his judicial philosophy was "out of the mainstream." The hearings dragged on for days and then weeks, like the most un-athletic Olympics the world has ever seen.

Then, a turning point: On September 23, Biden called former Chief Justice Warren Burger to testify. Burger was appointed by Nixon, and therefore was no bleeding-heart liberal. He supported Bork, saying that in the fifty years of his legal career, he had never seen a more qualified candidate. He seemed like an unlikely (and unwise) witness for Biden to call.

But Biden was more thoroughly prepared than anyone realized. He quoted Chief Justice Burger's own words, from years before: "The right of privacy . . . appear[s] nowhere in the Constitution or Bill of Rights; yet these important and unenumerated and unarticulated rights have nonetheless been found to share Constitutional protection with explicit guarantees."

It's a bit of a weedy quote, and Biden (rightly) realized that he needed to hit the point harder. Sharper. He needed to press the case. Biden looked up at the former chief justice. "Mr. Justice, that is what this debate is all about, at least with Judge Bork and I. And I wonder if you could speak with us a little bit, educate us a little bit, about these unenumerated rights—the right of privacy?"

Burger politely said that while he wasn't there to give a lecture on Constitutional law, "I see no problem with that statement, and I would be astonished if Judge Bork would not subscribe to it."

Wait. What?

Nixon's former chief justice—and a key Bork booster—had just contradicted Bork's position in the linchpin of the entire proceedings.

It was happening. The kid from Syracuse Law School was winning. It took weeks of tedium, but Biden kept hammering home the point—literally, with his gavel—that Bork was out of the mainstream. The moderate senators (including Republicans) were now swayed: *Bork's America is not our America.*

Finally, on October 23, 1987, the Senate was ready for its vote. A heated debate raged until the very last second. Outraged Republicans complained that the entire process had been a sham, that special interest groups were playing politics.

Biden, who felt he had done cartwheels to ensure fairness, gave a fiery rebuttal. Standing on the Senate floor, making eye contact with his colleagues, he came just short of yelling. "I asked Judge Bork, do you think you got a fair hearing? He said yes."

"Anything else you want to say, Judge Bork?"

"No."

"Anything at all you want to clarify?"

"No."

Joe Biden had brought it home. The Senate soon voted . . . and it wasn't close. 42 ayes, 58 nays. And thus a new verb was born into the political lexicon: "Borked."

Afterward, in a moment of hard-fought triumph, Biden's team had bottles of champagne and was ready to pop the corks. Biden killed the party before it started. "There's nothing here to celebrate," he told them. "There's a guy sitting at home whose whole life has been devoted toward being on the Supreme Court. Imagine how he feels."

WISDOM OF JOE

Classy in defeat, classy in victory.

The legal community golf-clapped in approval. "After [Biden] withdrew from the race, gracefully ... he turned his attention to the constitutional debate in recent years, and acquitted himself superbly," wrote the *Legal Times*. And the *New York Times* said that the hearings "instructed all of us on the Court and the Constitution. They have confounded the cynical view that everyone in Washington has base political motives."

After dropping out of the race, Joe Biden would not be Ronald Reagan's successor. Yet in one sense, at least, he proved to be something just as important: his counterpart. Reagan soon summoned Biden to the Oval Office to discuss the next Supreme Court justice. As Biden later described in his memoir, Reagan oozed charm and charisma.

"Hi, Joe," Reagan said, shaking hands. "Congratulations on Bork."

"No, Mr. President. There's no cause for congratulations. I feel bad for Judge Bork. He was a good man."

"Ah, he wasn't all that much," Reagan said with a smile, which Biden found befuddling. *Wasn't all that much?* Reagan then asked him, "Who do you want, Joe?"

"Mr. President, that's not my job."

Then, in a spirit of bipartisan collaboration (how quaint), Reagan cracked open his short list of Supreme Court nominees and asked

Biden for his thoughts. He gave one name, then another, then another. Then he got to the fifth name on his list: Anthony Kennedy. The president was curious: *Whattya think, Joe?*

Within weeks, Anthony Kennedy glided through the Senate, passing 97 to 0. By most accounts, Biden deserves credit for swapping Bork for Kennedy. "Joe Biden played a more consequential role in the history of the Supreme Court than almost any senator in American history," suggests the *New Yorker*'s legal expert, Jeffrey Toobin. "If Biden never did another thing as a senator than protect the nation from Robert Bork as a Supreme Court Justice, he will have a more significant, and noble, legacy than many presidential candidates."

In the last thirty years, think of how many Supreme Court decisions came down to the swing vote of Anthony Kennedy. To quickly channel *It's a Wonderful Life*, what would the world look like if Bork was on the Court?

"I have no real doubt that, had Bork been confirmed, the Court would never have decided to reaffirm the core holding of *Roe v. Wade* in *Planned Parenthood of [Southeastern] Pennsylvania v. Casey* or to overrule *Bowers v. Hardwick* in *Lawrence v. Texas*," says Larry Tribe, the constitutional scholar. He then spells out the jaw-dropping repercussions. "So abortion rights would have been jettisoned by the early 1990s if not sooner, and rights of sexual privacy would not have been constitutionalized. Same-sex marriage wouldn't be a constitutional right today. And every use of race by state and federal institutions to increase diversity in education and other realms would be flatly forbidden. In nearly all the 5–4 decisions in which Justice Kennedy joined four more liberal justices to create a majority, the Court would have gone the other way. The difference for women and marginalized groups would have been enormous." Without Joe Biden swinging his gavel in 1987, we might live in a very different America.

In the bittersweet aftermath of the Bork highs and election lows, an overworked Biden hit the gym to blow off some steam. While pumping iron he felt a shard of pain in his neck. *Must be a muscle pull*, he thought. Later that day, on Amtrak, he felt the pain again. Then he felt the pain in his legs. Then more pain in his neck. He saw a doctor who told him that he likely pulled a nerve while lifting weights, and gave Biden a neck brace.

Despite the awkward neck brace, Joe Biden had every reason to feel pretty good about himself. He had won a real victory with Bork. He still had Delaware—he would always have Delaware. His pollster called him to say, "The good news is that 74 percent of the people of Delaware think you ought to run for president again. . . . The bad news is that 43 percent of the people in Delaware think you're too arrogant."

"Find those people!" Biden said, laughing. "Find those people! Who are those people? I'm not too arrogant!" Biden was just forty-five years old, he had Jill and Hunter and Beau and Ashley, and he still had his beloved Corvette Stingray. Sure, 1988 might belong to Michael Dukakis, but who's to say Biden wasn't the future of the Democratic Party? He had time. He had lots of time.

In February of 1988, he felt even better when he spoke to a crowd at the University of Rochester, who, giving him a hero's welcome, kept him talking and talking and talking for a Q&A session of four hours. (This is the very same gabfest, in fact, where staffers had to cut off the microphones to get him to leave.) That night he flopped on his hotel bed, exhausted, hungry. He thought about ordering pizza.

Then he blacked out.

He woke up on the floor. He stared at the alarm clock. 4:10 a.m. Panic. It was hard to think. Hard to move. *Did he just have a heart attack?* He was dizzy, sick, nauseous. He could barely stand. He staggered to the bathroom and tried to force himself to vomit. Nothing came out. So he went back to bed and lay there, in agony, for hours.

The next morning, Biden tried to gut it out and make his scheduled flight. He told his staffers that he was fine, just a little sick, and that if he could get home, he'd be all right. "Can you carry my briefcase?" Biden asked a friend. (This was wildly out of character and it raised red flags; Biden always carried his own briefcase.)

Pretty soon his team figured out something was drastically wrong and hurried him to a local hospital. The doctors spotted blood in his spinal fluid. The likely diagnosis? A brain aneurysm.

Biden had zero margin for error. They needed to transfer him to Walter Reed hospital and wanted to use a helicopter, but a bumpy ride in a chopper could rupture the vessel and kill him. Instead they drove him in an ambulance, through the snow. A police escort led the way, with Beau in the front car, looking out for his pops.

Jill joined him in the ambulance and tried to lighten the mood. "You know, Joe, you always screw everything up," she said to him. "We were supposed to be going to a spa for Valentine's Day."

At the hospital they scanned his brain. He had an intracranial aneurysm, and he needed surgery ASAP. Especially in 1988, the surgery was aggressive and risky.

"Doc, what are my chances?" Biden asked, just before the surgery.

There were two neurosurgeons in the room. One of them paused, then asked Biden to clarify: "Senator, for mortality or morbidity?"

Mortality or morbidity. There was the chance that he would die, and then the chance that even if he lived, he would be seriously disabled, or technically "morbid."

"Let me put it to you this way," said Biden. "What are my chances of getting off this table and being completely normal?"

"Well, your chances of *living* are a lot better."

"Okay. What are they?"

"Thirty-five to fifty percent."

Then there was the added risk of morbidity: Paralysis. Loss of speech.

Loss of speech? For Joe Biden? "I think I laughed out loud when [the doctor] said that," Biden later remembered. "I kind of wish that had happened [before the election]."

It was almost time. Just before the surgery, Joe took a moment to look Beau and Hunter in the eyes, and say the words that he needed to say. "I guarantee you," he told them, "every single time you have a problem, when you have a tough decision to make, you look: I'll be there with you. Every time."

Jill and the family headed to a waiting room. Then Joe went under the knife. The doctors shaved his head, dressed the bald skull, flipped on the saw, and then cut into his brain.

===

IN THE WAITING ROOM, the family sat and prayed, hoped, worried. Beau and Hunter must have felt the way their father had, fifteen years earlier, when he waited to see if they would survive the car crash.

More waiting. The doctors had said that the operation should take around four hours, maybe four and a half.

Four hours—no word.

Five hours—no word.

Six.

Seven.

Eight.

Joe Biden's brain was under that knife for *nine hours*. Finally, the doctor reappeared . . . and said that it had gone well. Quite well. "The timing, I think, was appropriate," he told them.

The "timing," in fact, was terrifying: The aneurysm had exploded literally seconds after they had pried open his skull. (It's possible that the invasion of the knife itself had caused the burst, but still.)

Finally, Biden regained consciousness. Opened his eyes. At first he still had no idea if he was paralyzed, if he could speak, if he could still be Joe Biden. "He worked his fingers and toes under the sheet. Brought a hand up to touch his nose. Blinked his eyes. Saw the clock. Told himself the time, and figured the duration of his unconsciousness. He estimated the square footage of the ceiling by multiplying the tiles," writes Cramer. "He could think. He could move. He could talk. Thank God."

His skull was naked, bald, and coated in staples. He stayed at Walter Reed for a full ten days. The recovery wasn't easy, and it wasn't a given. Doctors hooked a titanium filter to his affected artery to avoid clotting in his lungs. It seemed to Biden that every few hours, the doctors were testing, pulling blood, or sticking angiogram injections into "a tender part of my groin."

Biden would live. And then it hit him: *Dropping out of the '88 election saved my life.* Jill had the same thought. If he had been campaigning for president, then he likely would have been wooing votes in New Hampshire, in the snow, and if he had collapsed there, he would have been too far away from the life-saving surgery at Walter Reed.

When he was discharged from the hospital, he faced the usual swarm of reporters. "I've asked you all to come today," he joked, "because I've decided to announce that I am reentering the race for president."

===== **WISDOM OF JOE** =====

Heal with humor.

Yet he was still woozy, still not himself. He was so frail that Jill forbade visitors or phone calls. (Among the callers was Ronald Reagan. He called twice but did not get through either time.)

Biden later went back for follow-up surgery. As he was wheeled into the operating room, he clutched a set of rosary beads, which the hospital usually didn't allow. The operation went fine, but he was stuck in the hospital for nearly a month. He spent most of his days in isolation, boredom, and sleep. It was hard to think. He lost a scary amount of weight, couldn't move the right side of his face, and had a drooping eyelid. The doctors thought the eyelid might stay that way. At least he had support from his well-wishers, including a note that read, "Dear Joe: What a smart guy! Everyone always said that anyone who goes into politics ought to have his head examined. And thank God you took it seriously."

Soon came the rumors: *Biden was a vegetable.* Biden tried to avoid being seen in public, self-conscious about his half-paralyzed face; when Jill dragged him to the ballet, they didn't go to their seats until after the theater had darkened.

Yet he was a Biden, and he remembered what his father had said. *When you're knocked down, get back up.*

Get up!

Get up!

So he rested, he rehabbed, and soon he began to feel like himself. Brother Jimmy gave him an archery set—Joe Biden! An archer!—so he began to use his bow and arrow. He drove his beloved car. He started smacking golf balls.

And at the end of this training montage, he put on a suit and tie, hopped in the car with Jill and the fam', and drove to one of his favorite places in the world: the Amtrak station.

It was his first day back, and the Amtrak crew welcomed him with signs and balloons. Even the train gave Biden an extra whistle of a salute.

Would Biden ever be the same? He addressed the issue squarely at the Sussex County jamboree, where he spoke to a crowd of seven hundred supporters. The crowd chanted. "Joe, Joe, Joe!"

Biden looked at the crowd and gave his first speech in a full seven months. "The good news is that I can do anything I did before," he told them. "The bad news is that I can't do anything better."

6

It's On Us (1988—94)

*"You're a coward for raising a hand to a woman or child—
and you're complicit if you fail to condemn it."*

IN 1989, NOW FULLY RECOVERED from his surgery, Biden shook with anger as he saw the news from Canada.

On a university campus in Montreal, a man named Marc Lépine walked into a classroom. He carried a semiautomatic hunting rifle.

"I want the women," he told the students, holding his gun.

He lined up the women against a wall.

"You're all a bunch of feminists!" he yelled. "I hate feminists."

He shot the first woman. Then the second. Soon he had shot and killed fourteen women. Then he killed himself.

Like everyone who saw the story, Joe Biden was horrified by what would become known as the Montreal Massacre. Yet something else caught his eye—as one of his staffers pointed out, if this had happened in the United States, technically, it wouldn't count as a hate crime.

Huh? How is that not a hate crime, *for Pete's sake?*

Biden dug a little deeper, and then he learned that, as one Supreme Court clerk explained, for violence to count as a hate crime, it needs to target a "victim's race, ethnicity, religion, or sexual orientation. . . . If a woman is beaten, raped, or killed because she is a woman, this is not considered a crime of hate," a legal technicality that's "welcome to no one but the misogynist."

That's a bunch of malarkey, Biden must have thought. (Quick context: If something is a hate crime, it counts as a violation of civil rights, which gives the victims more protection, and lets them sue in federal court.) The more he learned, the angrier he got.

Biden had been a tough-on-crime guy since the mid-'80s, and he made it a habit to track crime statistics. He noticed something strange: In the previous ten years, violent crimes against men had dropped, but crimes against women had surged. Biden did more research. One appalling survey showed that in the United States, one in ten men thought that it was "okay for a husband to beat his wife if she doesn't obey him." *One in ten.* The math was grim; with 53 million married couples in 1990, this meant that 5 million women were at risk.

He asked one of his staffers, Victoria Nourse, to hit the books and gather more data. "He wanted to hear what a woman had to say about it," Nourse says. "And this is the thing about Joe Biden. Although he is known for his loquacious behavior, he *listens.*" Biden and Nourse drilled deeper, spoke to victims, and then held a series of hearings to show that *this issue matters, damn it.* They provided a platform for victims to come forward and share their stories. One of these women was a college student who had been sexually assaulted by her friend's boyfriend. Her dorm's RA later told her, "You were raped."

"No I wasn't. I *knew* him," she told the RA.

That was the mind-set about rape. That was the culture. More women came forward. In one case, the judge "suggested that a rape victim had invited the attack by wearing a crocheted miniskirt." (As Biden said, "The stupidity was infuriating.")

So Biden began his work on what would become, in time, the Violence Against Women Act (VAWA). It seems crazy that this bill was controversial. Who's *against* the victims of sexual assault? Yet consider the senator from Alabama, Jeremiah Denton, who seemed fuzzy on why marital rape would be considered a crime. "Damn it," he said, "when you get married, you kind of expect you're going to get a little sex."

It was not easy to muscle a bill through Congress. It took time. So Biden buckled down, just like he had with Bork. He called in experts. He demanded more research.

He urged others to understand that violence against women affects *all* women, not just the specific victims. Biden understood "the lack of control that is experienced not only by women who are themselves victims but by all the women who have to constrain their daily activities to avoid being a victim," and that, therefore, "violence against women deprives women of equality," said Sally Goldfarb, who had helped create the bill.

In 1990, Biden tried to get the bill passed.

Not enough votes.

In 1991, he tried again.

Not enough votes.

He kept working on the bill, but he would soon be forced to deal with a new distraction: a potential Supreme Court nominee named Clarence Thomas.

IN 1991, ONCE AGAIN, Biden was the chairman of the Judiciary Committee. Once again, Joe Biden would swing his gavel and frame the debate and set the tempo. And once again, Joe Biden zeroed in on that age-old question of the right to privacy.

Things began innocently enough. A quick snapshot of the early days:

Clarence Thomas *did* believe there was "a right to privacy in the Fourteenth Amendment."

"Well, Judge," Biden asked, "does that right to privacy . . . protect the right of a woman to decide for herself in certain instances whether or not to terminate a pregnancy?"

Clarence Thomas was no sucker. Perhaps he had watched the Bork tapes—okay, he had *certainly* watched the Bork tapes—so he tried to say as little as possible, admitting only that when it came to *Roe v. Wade*, "I do not think that at this time I could maintain my impartiality as a member of the judiciary and comment on that specific case."

In other words, *No comment.* He had parried Biden's move. It's just like how in *The Karate Kid*, Daniel-san's "crane kick" defeated Cobra Kai and won him the trophy, but it failed him in *The Karate Kid II*.

"You will be pleased to know I don't want to know anything about abortion," Biden said, but hey, why use ten words when a thousand will do? He quickly added, "I don't want to know how you think about abortion. I don't want to know whether you have ever thought about abortion. I don't want to know whether you ever even discussed it. I don't want to know whether you have talked about it in your sleep. I don't want to know anything about abortion."

The pundits rolled their eyes. "Biden's queries were sometimes so long and convoluted that Thomas would forget what the question was," write Jane Mayer and Jill Abramson in *Strange Justice*. "Biden had considered the Bork hearings his finest hour, a high-minded discourse that had engaged the country. Bork was defeated fairly, in Biden's view, because of his legal opinions. This time Biden's questions seemed occasionally to be a vehicle to show off his legal acumen rather than to elicit answers." (What's that old adage about the sequel never being as good as the original?)

So far, though, let's speak plainly—*YAWN*. This is all a bit dry. It's more C-SPAN than HBO. If the Clarence Thomas hearings had ended right there, then the world might have moved on, and Biden would have pivoted back to his Violence Against Women Act.

The hearings didn't end there.

Enter Anita Hill.

At the time a professor of commercial law at the University of Oklahoma, Anita Hill had worked for Thomas a decade earlier. Over the phone, she told the Judiciary Committee—Biden's committee—that she was sexually harassed by Clarence Thomas, but she wanted to remain anonymous.

From the jump, Biden faced some tough choices. Should he grant the request for anonymity? Force her to go public? (Quick clarification: At this point, Thomas was simply being considered by the fourteen-member Judiciary Committee, which would then make a "favorable" or "unfavorable" recommendation, and then Thomas would go before the full Senate either way. That's how it always works. Back in 1987, Biden's committee had sent Bork to the Senate floor with a 9–5 "unfavorable" recommendation.)

Hill wrote a detailed memo that laid out the allegations, which was then read by the committee. One of the committee members, Senator Arlen Specter, a Republican, called Clarence Thomas directly to get his take. According to Specter, Thomas said, "No, sir, with God as my witness . . . it just didn't happen. I wouldn't do that. . . . Black men are always accused of that. . . . Never happened, absolutely not." Specter then wrote, "African American men are often described sexually in terms of prowess and size, and as predators. He told me how painful it was for him to hear Hill's charges, and how untrue and extraordinary they were."

Sexual harassment. Race. Gender. This was explosive stuff, and it would be easy to get it wrong. Let's say you're in Biden's shoes. What do you do? The tricky thing is that Hill, at that point, had no desire to go public with her accusations. It would be a big risk, and would mean putting herself in a position where it was her word against a very powerful man's word—and the cards were stacked against her.

So should Biden force Hill to testify, or let the vote go forward, with most of the Senate unaware of the charges? Biden ultimately decided that since Hill was unwilling to come forward publicly, it wasn't fair to punish Thomas with an anonymous charge.

The timing was dreadful. The committee was scheduled to vote, so Biden said they should vote. When it was his turn, Biden said that he would not support Thomas for reasons of legal substance (the right to privacy), but, "for this Senator, there is no question with respect to the nominee's character."

The committee voted. It was a 7–7 tie—so no recommendation, favorable or unfavorable—and then this live grenade was tossed to the Senate floor.

"I must start off with a presumption of giving the person accused the benefit of the doubt," Biden said in the chamber. "I must seek the truth and I must ask straightforward and tough questions, and in my heart I know if that woman is telling the truth it will be almost unfair to her. On the other hand, if I don't ask legitimate questions, then I am doing a great injustice to someone who might be totally innocent. It's a horrible dilemma because you have two lives at stake here."

Should Biden delay the start of the full Senate hearings, which would give more time for everyone to take stock of the charges of sexual harassment? He decided not to. Civil rights groups were appalled—*Shouldn't we take more time?* Others asked even tougher questions. "What disturbs me as much as the allegations themselves is that the Senate appears not to take the charge of sexual harassment seriously," said Senator Barbara Mikulski, one of only two women in the entire Senate. (The other was Nancy Kassebaum.) *Ninety-eight of the one hundred senators were men.* Most of them white. Neither of the two women sat on the Judiciary Committee.

Biden soon gave Hill a call directly. According to Hill's book *Speaking Truth to Power*, over the phone, Biden advised her that she get a good lawyer.

"I wish I weren't the chairman. I'd come to be your lawyer," said Biden, as Hill remembers. She wrote, "I could almost see him flashing his instant smile to convince both of us that the experience would be agreeable."

The experience would not be agreeable. In his opening remarks to the full Senate, Biden explained that this was not a "trial" but a "fact-finding hearing." He acknowledged that achieving fairness in the charged atmosphere "may be the most difficult task I have ever undertaken in my close to nineteen years in the U.S. Senate. . . . It will be easy and perhaps understandable for the witnesses [e.g., Anita Hill] to fear unfair treatment, but it is my job, as chairman, to ensure as best as I possibly can fair treatment, and that is what I intend to do."

The play-by-play has been extensively covered elsewhere, so we won't reenact the whole drama, but it's important to remember the following: This was on TV. The entire nation was watching. At the time, workplace harassment was barely on the public's radar, and now a woman, an African American woman, was accusing a powerful man of sexual harassment at a time when some senators were saying, openly, that it was okay to rape your wife.

Okay, on that note, let's dive in.

Summarizing the case for Thomas (read: *against* Anita Hill), eighty-eight-year-old Senator Strom Thurmond argued that out of a hundred prior witnesses, not one "had one disparaging comment to make about Clarence Thomas's moral character," and the "alleged harassment she describes took place some ten years ago." (Counterpoint: The behavior is still inexcusable. Sexual harassment is not like milk. It doesn't expire.)

Thomas denied everything, making the case that *he* was the victim, and that the charges had done a "grave and irreparable injustice" to his family. "Confirm me if you want, don't confirm me if you are so led, but let this process end. Let me and my family regain our lives. I never asked to be nominated. It was an honor. Little did I know the price, but it is too high."

Hill took the stand. At this point she had already become the target of insults, smears, and questions about her motivations. "It is only after a great deal of agonizing consideration and sleepless nights that I am able to talk of these unpleasant matters to anyone but my close friends," Hill said, and then launched into what had happened. She explained that Thomas asked her out. She said no. He kept asking her out. She kept saying no. The details were vivid, pornographic, and uncomfortable.

To boost their case for Clarence Thomas, a few of the senators would latch on to only one strategy: vilify Anita Hill. Arlen Specter charged that Hill was guilty of "flat-out perjury." Senator Orrin Hatch had a theory: Maybe she made up the entire story, based on the plot of *The Exorcist*? And Senator Howard Metzenbaum said, "If that's sexual harassment, half the senators on Capitol Hill could be accused."

Even though she was not required to do so, Hill took a lie detector test.

She aced it.

Yet Biden, as chairperson, said the test should not be considered. "If we get to the point in this country where lie detector tests are the basis upon which we make judgments," he argued, "we have reached a sad day for the civil liberties of this country." (The logic has merit, but still . . . Hill aced a lie detector test, and it's inadmissible?)

To both simplify and complicate matters, Anita Hill was not the only woman who accused Clarence Thomas of sexual harassment. Other women stepped forward, such as Angela Wright. Yet none of them testified in person before the Senate, a fact that remains controversial.

Biden insists that he had welcomed Angela Wright to testify. "[T]here's a myth that's grown up that we somehow denied her," Biden told Jules Witcover in 2009. "We had her in town to testify, we expected her to testify, we prepared her to testify; she chose not to testify. She had her own reasons. I don't know exactly what they were. And people say, well, why didn't you have her testify anyway? Well, that's like calling a hostile witness in a case." There's evidence to back him up. A letter dated October 13, 1991, corroborates his statement. "If you want to testify at the hearing in person, I will honor that request," he writes.

Biden has also been criticized for not calling in more expert witnesses, people who could help inform the Senate—and educate America—about sexual harassment. Biden says he wanted to do just that. "I wanted a panel on sexual harassment to come and testify, so we could put in context what we were talking about," he said in 1994. "And it was decided by the Hill people that they didn't want that panel to come on. Again, there was a feeling—communicated to me secondhand—that Anita Hill had won this thing. She had made her case. And I kept saying, 'Wrong, this ain't over.' I was very disappointed."

There would be no expert witnesses. There would be no in-person testimony from the other women who accused Thomas of sexual harassment, which clearly would have buttressed Hill's allegations. (*Written* testimony was admitted, but did that have the same impact?)

The Senate confirmed Thomas 52 to 48, and that was that. Would he have squeaked through if the other women were allowed to testify? Or if the hearings had been given more time? Or if a panel of experts had testified? And how much should we blame Biden for the way Hill was treated?

Years later, Hill spoke about what she saw as Biden's failure in the hearings. "I think he did two things that were a disservice to me, that were a disservice more importantly to the public," Hill said in a 2014 interview. "There were three women who were ready and waiting and subpoenaed to be giving testimony about similar behavior that they had experienced or witnessed. He failed to call them."

She continued. "There also were experts who could have given real information as opposed to the misinformation that the Senate was giving . . . and helped the public understand sexual harassment. He failed to call them." At the time, a Biden spokesperson responded simply: "The Vice President continues to wish nothing but the best for Anita Hill." (In Biden's 365-page memoir, *Promises to Keep*, the name Anita Hill appears exactly 0 times.)

On the other hand, some argue that Biden has gotten a bad rap. "Then-Senator Biden felt that he had an obligation to try to sit in a neutral position as chair, and that was his priority—presenting a fair hearing," his counsel on the Judiciary Committee, Cynthia Hogan, later argued. "I don't think anyone was happy with the hearings. I think then-Senator Biden was surprised by the way the Republicans went on the attack. . . . It wasn't that he didn't take sexual harassment seriously." Joe Biden, like the nation, seemed to be grappling with the proper way to address sexual harassment, how to put it in the right context, and how to understand it. He was learning. And in the end, he did try to give Hill a full-throated defense. "There is absolutely not one shred of evidence to suggest that Professor Hill is fantasizing," he said on the Senate floor, steel in his voice, scolding his colleagues. "There is no shred of evidence for the garbage I hear . . . that the only answer we can come up with is that she must be fantasizing. . . . So I hope you will drop this stereotypical malarkey."

At least one thing is crystal clear: Anita Hill's life would never be the same. "I am no longer an anonymous, private individual—my name having become synonymous with sexual harassment," she writes in *Speaking Truth to Power*. "To my supporters I represent the courage to come forward and disclose a painful truth—a courage which thousands of others have found since the hearing. To my detractors I represent the debasement of a public forum, at best, a pawn, at worst, a perjurer. Living with these conflicting perceptions is difficult, sometimes overwhelming."

===

IN 1991, PATRICIA IRELAND was the acting president of the National Organization of Women (NOW). "This is not to say that there's anything *good* about the Thomas hearings," she says, "but there were a whole lot of women in this country who saw the hearings, and who had experienced sexual harassment, and started talking about it. And then there were men who loved these women, and they heard these stories, and they started talking about it. Husbands, brothers, fathers. There was an explosion of public consciousness." Her NOW offices received so many calls that she had to install a new switchboard. She says it's not a coincidence that 1992 would be labeled "The Year of the Woman," with the election of four women U.S. senators: Barbara Boxer, Patty Murray, Carol Moseley Braun, and Dianne Feinstein.

Something else seemed to change, too: There was more willingness to talk about domestic violence against women. Biden's staffer charged with spearheading the Violence Against Women Act, Victoria Nourse, says she noticed the shift. "The country changed, and the Senate changed, after Anita Hill," says Nourse. "Women made themselves quite clear—*that [hearing] was a mess.*" She says that helped open the minds, and ears, of other male senators. The votes were more gettable. In the background, Biden's team had continued work on what would become a three-year investigation into the deeper causes of violence against women. They hatched a report designed to evoke real emotions, and to focus on something specific: *Violence Against Women: A Week in the Life of America*, with involvement from both Democratic senators (including Ted Kennedy) and Republicans (including Orrin Hatch).

The report was unflinching. It found that in 1991, there were at least 21,000 domestic crimes against women ... *every week*. "These figures reveal a total of at least 1.1 million assaults, aggravated assaults, murders, and rapes against women committed in the home and reported to the police," Biden writes in the introduction. Yet he knew that statistics alone wouldn't shake people to act. He wanted to look at "the human face" behind the numbers. From the report:

- A twenty-six-year-old Connecticut woman is attacked by her boyfriend of five years; he breaks her right arm with a hammer.
- A forty-six-year-old New Mexico woman is beaten and pushed out of a moving car by her husband. She spends three days in the hospital recovering from a broken tailbone and other injuries.

- A Texas woman is stabbed in her apartment by a stranger who enters through sliding glass doors in the middle of the night.

This gruesome report ran twenty pages. Biden says that if his team included every event they knew about, the report would run seven thousand pages. Sometimes Joe Biden can goof around, and sometimes—likely more than we know—he's deadly serious. "What do these stories tell us? At the most basic level, they tell us that no one is immune," Biden writes. "Violence happens to young women and old women, to rich women and poor women, to homeless women and working women."

The Violence Against Women Act included $300 million to train police, prosecutors, and victim advocates to help survivors, fund education programs, and toughen prosecutions of abusers. It also helped define sexual assault as a hate crime, letting women bring civil suits against their attackers.

Cynics might think of the VAWA as a PR move, a way to atone for his role in the Anita Hill testimony. Only one problem with this theory: Biden launched this crusade in 1990, and he had already tried, twice, to get the bill through Congress, even before the world had heard of Clarence Thomas.

He tried again to get the law passed in 1992.

Not enough votes.

1993.

Not enough votes.

Finally, in 1994, he cracked the logjam. All those years cultivating friendships with Republicans had paid off. People trusted him. "Everyone knew that it was *personal* for him," says Nourse. He listened to the victim hotlines, talked to survivors, and heard more stories of abuse.

"[Republicans] knew that he wasn't going to let the crime bill forward if they took it [VAWA] out. And it wouldn't have happened if he didn't have that strong moral compass." To secure Republican support, Biden bundled the VAWA with the $30.2 billion Violent Crime Control and Law Enforcement Act, which put 100,000 cops on the street. If that sounds like a mouthful, you can remember it by what senators called it at the time—the "Biden Crime Bill." Biden is proud of the win. (The nuance, like always, is complicated. According to some, the bill led to a stunning long-term drop in murders and other violent crimes. According to others, it accelerated the nation's incarceration problem, and disproportionately hurt minority communities. The debate is not simple.)

When President Clinton inked the legislation into law, the Democratic majority leader said that Biden was "the one person most responsible for passage of this bill," calling him "the most underrated legislator, the most effective legislator in the Senate, bar none."

Most underrated legislator. Most effective legislator. Biden was no longer the golden boy. He was no longer the young vision of hope, the silver-tongued orator, or the guy with a spotless record. He now had bruises. Graying hair. The scars of politics, the scars of bad PR, and the physical scars from life-threatening surgery. Yet with the passage of the Violence Against Women Act and the crime bill—along with his globe-trotting work on the Foreign Relations Committee (more on that soon)—he seemed to relish his role as a senatorial *doer*, not just a talker.

It had taken more than four years for the bill to become a law. But Biden stuck with it.

WISDOM OF JOE

Play the long game.

"When I look at Biden and the Anita Hill hearings, this is the lesson, for me: People are complex. I see that people make mistakes, and they make huge mistakes," says Patricia Ireland, the former president of NOW. "I don't want to be held to who I was in 1991. I've grown and learned and changed since then." She pauses, thinks. "But Joe Biden came back. He didn't go hide in a corner. He didn't go feel sorry for himself. He just doubled down on doing good work, pushing hard on issues that affect women's lives. And that goes a long way for me. He gets credit for persistence and determination over a long number of years."

The most important legacy of the VAWA, says Ireland, is that it helped *change the culture* about the way we think about these issues. "Whether it was sexual harassment, physical harassment, sexual assault, or violence in families—that was a *shame* that you didn't talk about, a private matter, a family matter. You looked the other way," says Ireland. "Biden was part of changing that perception to say, *No, that's not a problem that an individual woman has. It's a structural problem. It's a cultural problem.*"

Biden's work did not stop with the Violence Against Women Act. He would spend the next twenty-five years working to further change that culture, spreading awareness about sexual assault, and how it was not just a "women's issue," but one that needs to be owned by the men, too. *It's not just on women . . . it's on us.* Whether the crime is the Montreal Massacre, domestic violence, sexual harassment, or sexual assault on campus—it's on men to look the evil in the eye, to do the right thing. (Is it a coincidence that Biden saw his colleagues tear into Anita Hill, while too many men stayed silent?) "You're a coward for raising a hand to a woman or child—and you're complicit if you fail to condemn it," he said in 2014, on the twentieth anniversary of the VAWA. He then worked with President Obama to launch an initiative—to fight sexual assault, to educate, to get men on board—that he continues to champion to this day: *It's On Us.*

7

Second Chances (1991–2008)

*"And I absolutely can say, with certainty,
I would not be anybody's vice president, period."*

DECADES AGO, WHEN HE WAS seventeen years old and in the backyard of his friend's house, Joe Biden had said, "Mr. Walsh, I want to be president of the United States."

True ambition might wax and wane, but it is never extinguished. In the years since passing the Violence Against Women Act, Biden would keep toiling, keep Amtraking, and keep fighting for the little guy. (By one estimate, he logged more than 2 million miles on Amtrak.) And he knew there was one important thing he could do that would buttress his grander ambitions: master foreign policy.

"I've met with virtually every leader in the world," Biden is fond of pointing out. "I know these guys." These foreign adventures began in 1979, when he was still a rookie with that full head of dark hair, tagging along on a trip to Yugoslavia.

His traveling companion? Averell Harriman, the legendary diplomat. Harriman had been at the Yalta Conference next to Stalin,

Churchill, and FDR and later drove the Marshall Plan. Not a bad mentor.

They talked shop on the flight to Yugoslavia, where they were to meet with Josip Broz Tito, the eighty-seven-year-old dictator. Harriman—Biden's Yoda—gave him two key lessons. One: *Go and see for yourself.* Don't just read newspapers or accept conventional wisdom; use your own eyes and ears. Two: *Don't trust, but engage.* Tito was nominally a Communist, but he fought like hell to keep Yugoslavia *out* of the Soviet tractor beam. "By keeping up relations with leaders like Tito," Biden later wrote, "we could nudge them toward change."

The lessons stuck—for years Biden would personally visit hot zones, gather intel, and visit both troops and generals, presidents and peasants. And something else stuck: Biden's fascination with Yugoslavia. As a dictator, Tito had a clenched grip on the uneasy alliance of Serbs, Muslims, Croats, Bosnians, Kosovars, and Slovenes. Then Tito died. Order collapsed. In 1991, the power vacuum was filled by Slobodan Milošević, a Serb. Then, bloodshed.

Remembering Harriman's advice—*Go and see for yourself*—Biden visited Bosnia, Croatia, and Serbia and he saw the nightmare. He learned of mutilations, beatings, gang rapes, and the murder of little girls. The war is complex and awful and tragic and outside the scope of this book, but Biden was unafraid to call it what it was: genocide. An estimated 100,000 people would die.

He came back to the Senate, impassioned, to rally his colleagues to the cause. He prepared a thirty-six-page document with detailed recommendations of air strikes and policy proposals.

He couldn't muster enough support, as it's never easy to make the case for military action. He gave more speeches. Still nothing. "The West has dithered so pathetically, and Bosnia has suffered so terribly," Biden wrote in a 1993 op-ed in the *New York Times*. Biden's basic request: *Arm the victims.* He urged first George H. W. Bush, then Bill Clinton, to lift the UN embargo against Bosnia and send weapons to those who were getting slaughtered. (Quick perspective: Biden didn't just oppose George Bush, he squared off against Clinton, again putting principles ahead of party.)

"Biden opposed Clinton on Bosnia for three years. It wasn't easy," remembers Mike Haltzel, his senior foreign policy advisor at the time. "And we did it because it was the right thing to do." Biden hounded Clinton on the phone—four times a week—to try to change his mind. Once again Biden reached across the aisle, this time to Bob Dole, and together the two men championed the cause.

And in the heat of the conflict, Biden would eventually meet the man responsible for much of this bloodshed, Slobodan Milošević, in person. On a top-secret trip—secret, so Milošević couldn't use Biden's presence as his own propaganda—Biden wanted to take the measure of the man. Milošević showed Biden map after map, trying to convince him that there was no ethnic cleansing, no genocide. Biden saw through the bullshit. And he called him on it.

"What do you think of me?" Milošević asked him.

Biden looked him in the eyes. "I think you're a damn war criminal."

WISDOM OF JOE

Call a bully a bully.

It's a gross oversimplification to suggest that Biden was the only reason that Clinton, finally, moved to intervene. That said, "When you look back, Senator Biden got Bosnia right earlier than anyone," said James Rubin, one of Biden's policy advisors. "He understood that a combination of force and diplomacy would revive American leadership and avoid a disaster in Europe." As Biden ballparks it, the intervention saved 10,000 lives.

And Milošević? He was tried as a damn war criminal.

JOE THE NAME-BUTCHERER

Biden has an almost preternatural talent for making friends with strangers, schmoozing with world leaders, and charming the charmless.

Yet he does have one bit of diplomatic kryptonite.

"He's just *terrible* with names, especially in a foreign language," says Mike Haltzel. "I mean he just butchers things. If your name is not Johnson, you got a real problem."

Haltzel tells a story about a time when he and Biden traveled once again to Bosnia, in the late '90s, this time to meet with a woman named Biljana Plavšić, who was then president of the Republika Srpska. She was tough. And she would later serve for years as a war criminal. Haltzel knew it would be a difficult meeting. Looking back, he now says it was the most hostile meeting he ever attended with Biden on foreign soil. ("We had just bombed the crap out of them less than two years earlier.")

They met in Plavšić's office, which was more like a Serbian Orthodox church. Plavšić flanked herself with muscular Serbian generals (or as Haltzel puts it, "goons"), meant to intimidate. Haltzel knew that Biden had to have *something* positive to say—anything—to establish a sliver of rapport. He found an angle: Republika Srpska had just moved their capital from an ultra-fascist city, Pale, to a more cosmopolitan city, Banja Luka. *That's perfect.* Biden could congratulate her on the move of the nation's capital—a harmless courtesy, and one consistent with progressive values. So Haltzel suggested that as a conversational tactic.

"The problem is he's just not good with foreign words," says Haltzel, so in the briefing book, he had spelled it out "Pale" phonetically, using both italics and capitals. They got to the point of the meeting where Biden could tactfully bring up Pale. "So he starts to sink his teeth into it," says Haltzel.

Biden then congratulated Plavšić on the move from *Pele*, pronouncing it like the soccer player.

"He keeps talking about Pele and I'm thinking, *Oh Jesus Christ, what are we gonna do?*" says Haltzel. "I write down a note and I put, 'Pale is a Bosnian-Serb town. Pele was a Brazilian soccer player.'"

Haltzel later clarified that the gaffe did no damage and that the meeting was a success, but at that moment, he used some nonverbal cues to slip Biden the note. "I slid it over to him, and I can see him look at me. He came close to bursting out laughing."

———

KOSOVO. IRAQ. AFGHANISTAN. After forty-plus years of loafers-on-the-ground visits, few can top Biden's foreign policy bona fides. And after the Soviet Union collapsed, Biden helped lead the charge to expand NATO to include Poland, the Czech Republic, and Hungary. But it's fair to wonder, How involved was Joe Biden, *really*, in this process?

"Well, I'll give you a story," says Haltzel, who was once again in the center of the foreign policy action. "And when I tell the young staffers on the Hill this, their jaws drop." In 1998, the Foreign Relations Committee held debates on NATO expansion for seven straight days, morning to night, which is like March Madness for C-SPAN junkies. At the time, the Republicans controlled Congress, so Republican Jesse Helms served as the chairperson. "If you know anything about the Senate, every bill has a floor manager," says Haltzel. "And the floor manager determines which amendments will be considered, what order they'll be taken up, the order of speaking . . . everything. He or she basically runs the show. And this wasn't just any old bill. This was a treaty ratification. And it wasn't just any old treaty, but the most important ratification in sixty years."

Here's the wrinkle: "Jesse Helms, as chairman of the Foreign Relations Committee, should have been the floor manager, but Helms was not up to it intellectually or physically," says Haltzel. So he assumed that the Republicans would tap John McCain as floor manager, or maybe Republican Gordon Smith, from Oregon. "You know who they chose as manager? Joe Biden."

The *Republicans* chose Biden over one of their own. "It is absolutely incredible, and I tell staffers that and they just don't believe it. And that shows the confidence [Republicans] had in him, and it was simply just remarkable."

The final passage of the NATO enlargement was 80 to 19, which makes it look like a slam-dunk, a gimme. But the final vote overlooks some crucial nuance. "I mean, all the books that were written about first round NATO enlargement were just wrong," says Haltzel. "They said it was inevitable, it was gonna happen. The final passage was 80 to 19, but you needed sixty-six or sixty-seven, depending on how many people were there, to pass it. Biden himself must have convinced ten people. It could have been really nip and tuck. If he had gone the other way, I don't think it would have passed."

So why would the Republicans tap Biden to be the floor manager? There are a few reasons. The first, of course, is that he's likable as hell. He had buddies everywhere. For decades he had remembered birthdays, asked about kids, and broke bread with Republicans at lunch. And Republicans knew Biden had that moxie on the global stage (even if he couldn't nail the names). "He would greet the vice president of another country in the same way that he hails an old friend from Scranton," says videographer Arun Chaudhary, after seeing him in action. "With this understanding, familiarity, and unbelievable warmth."

Yet chummy gets you only so far. The deeper truth, and the one that doesn't grab many headlines or slingshot around Twitter, is that Biden had quietly, methodically done his homework and commanded all of the details. And his colleagues knew it, on both the Left and the Right.

Example: The main argument *against* ratification of the NATO treaty was one of cost. Would it cost the taxpayers more? So Biden threw himself into the economics of NATO, just as he did with the intellectual underpinnings of Bork. He had his team assemble a briefing book that was "probably twelve inches thick," remembers Haltzel. "Biden just took it as a matter of pride that he was gonna go back and look at all the cost factors, the infrastructural cost, what it would cost to build airfields, what it would cost the U.S. taxpayer. I mean, just every possible thing you could imagine. And he mastered it."

==

FEW CAN THROW STONES AT Biden's foreign policy cred, yet this is not to say that his record is spotless. He now has the unpleasant task of justifying how he voted *against* invading Iraq in 1990, then *for* invading Iraq in 2003, and then later *against* the troop surge in 2007. Debates can be had about each of these votes—and the nuance abounds—but you could make the case that he batted 0 for 3.

In the case of the first Iraq war, he argued, on principle, that the president needed congressional authority to go to war, and he cited the Constitution and the Founders, and more than twenty years before it was cool, he cited Alexander Hamilton. He would do so again in 1998, arguing, "On this point, the writings of Alexander Hamilton, a very strong defender ... of Presidential power, is very instructive. ... In Federalist 69, Hamilton emphasized that the President's power as Commander in Chief would be 'much inferior' to that of the British King, amounting to 'nothing more than the supreme command and direction of the military and naval forces.'"

Biden's point? The Framers—and Hamilton—didn't just want Congress to rubber-stamp the approval of a war, but actually have real teeth. So Biden tried to curb the president's wartime powers, an issue that goes back to Nixon and Vietnam. "The Founding Fathers had little interest, it seems, in the ceremonial aspects of war. The real issue was congressional authorization of war. ... Even in 1789—to quote Hamilton ..." and then he went on for a while, as he is wont to do.

And while we're speaking of that first Iraq war, even when Biden got things wrong, he seemed willing to take his lumps if it was good for America. He had voted against the war, and clearly, if Bush Senior failed, that would make him less likely to win re-election in 1992. (At the height of the Gulf War, Bush's approval rating soared to 89 percent.) Biden's reaction? *Excellent. Good for him.* "If the president successfully prosecutes the war, and I hope he does," he said, "that's worth losing the White House."

===== **WISDOM OF JOE** =====

Nation over party.

For twenty years, the timing was never quite right for another presidential charge of the light brigade. In 1992, Biden still had the odor of the plagiarism scandal and the Clarence Thomas hearings. The election of 1996, of course, belonged to Bubba. In 2000, Gore had dibs as the heir apparent. In 2004, in a moment of clear self-assessment, Biden read the political landscape and determined that it's "too much of a long shot."

Yet in 2008? Biden must have been thinking, *For Pete's sake, I've put in my time.*

And he didn't try to hide it. Biden did something that politicians are never supposed to do: He admitted that he wanted to be president. "It is my intention to seek the nomination," he said in 2005, more than three years before the election. "I know I'm supposed to be more coy with you."

In an echo of '88, once again, the Republicans had back-to-back terms in the White House, and after eight years of a guy "you could get a beer with," the Democrats were feeling bullish. In another echo of '88, Biden looked around at the other Democratic wannabes: John Edwards, Tom Vilsack, Dennis freakin' Kucinich. He outranked all of them. He outcharmed all of them. "I don't think John Edwards knows what the heck he is talking about," he said at the time. (Okay, so *Never neg*, at times, is more *Usually try not to neg*.)

Another candidate: Hillary Clinton. *Hmmmm.* Trickier.

And what about this new wild card, the junior senator from Illinois? The one with the funny name? In a 2007 interview, Biden said,

"I'd be a little surprised if he actually does run." He then suggested that Barack Obama was on "everyone's number-two list," as in an option for vice president. *Oh, Joe.*

In 2007, he made it official. "I am running for president. I'm going to be Joe Biden, and I'm going to try to be the best Biden I can be. If I can, I've got a shot. If I can't, I lose."

He knew it was a dicey gamble. So why do it? "He knew there was an easier life if he didn't run for president," explains Ted Kaufman, his longtime friend. "Jill agreed, but both of them were of the opinion that he had, really, a responsibility to try to do it. . . . Growing old is not a whole lot of fun, but one of the advantages of my age is you really can *try*. Joe Biden is the same way. What would he think of himself if he didn't even try to be president?"

It wasn't about power, fame, or legacy, says Kaufman. "I think a lot of it comes out of an obligation to serve. It's the same reason why Barack Obama didn't go to work on Wall Street when he got out of Harvard and went to work as a community organizer. It's an extension of that. It's all about how you are hardwired, about how important service is to you. And with Joe Biden, service is his life."

You have to feel for Biden. For decades he had worked and worked and worked to become, arguably, one of the most qualified presidential candidates in history. Who had more tenure? Who had more foreign policy experience? Who else had saved America from a Justice Bork? It must have been tough to see this up-and-coming crop of candidates promising hope and change. *That used to be my thing!*

Remember how, back in 1972, twenty-nine-year-old Joe Biden used to fill up high school gyms, thrill the teenagers, and get them to hand-deliver his campaign brochures? And then in the early '80s, he shot to semistardom with that youthful Kennedy moxie? Somehow, over the last twenty years, he had now become … old. Father Time remains undefeated.

Just listen to how he positioned himself: "I can stem the tide of this slide [in Iraq] and restore America's leadership in the world and change our priorities," he said on *Good Morning America*, outlining his case for the presidency. "I will argue that my experience and my track record, both on the foreign and the domestic side, put me in a position to be able do that."

America heard this and said, *Meh.* "Experience" was a flavor of ice cream that no one seemed to want. And "track record" just didn't have any sex appeal. For all Biden's years making cameos on the nightly news—Bork, Anita Hill, the Violence Against Women Act, Bosnia—he just couldn't crack the mainstream conversation. "The bottom line is that no one in the country knows me," he correctly said at the time. "They know Joe Biden if they watch Sunday morning shows or occasionally turn on C-SPAN. But absent that, they don't know much about me at all." The early polls had Barack Obama and Hillary Clinton way out in front, and then Biden polling under 5 percent.

But he had time; it was a long campaign. He would show the world just who Joe Biden really was. Maybe he could make his case, perhaps, in an early interview with the *New York Observer*? A reporter asked him for his thoughts on Clinton and Edwards, so Biden spoke about them extensively, and critically. Almost as an afterthought, he added a few words on Obama. "I mean, you got the first mainstream African American, who is articulate and bright and clean and a nice-looking guy. I mean, that's a storybook, man."

Sigh. This throwaway comment—intended as a compliment—was buried in the eleventh paragraph of the article. Yet it's the only quote that mattered. *Drudge Report* called it a "Biden Shocker." The *New York*

Times called it "A Bumpy Rollout for Biden." SEN. BIDEN STUMBLES OUT OF GATE IN '08 RACE, declared the *Wilmington News Journal*, Biden's hometown paper. Ezra Klein of *The American Prospect* said, "Bye Bye Biden."

People wanted to know: What the hell did "clean" and "articulate" mean? Was the implication that most African Americans were *not* clean and articulate? The next morning Biden told reporters that he was just referencing something his mom used to say: "Clean as a whistle, sharp as a tack."

That didn't cut it. He made one of his first appearances on *The Daily Show* and took another shot at an explanation. "What I was attempting to be, and not very artfully, is complimentary," he said. "The word that got me in trouble is using 'clean.' I should have said 'fresh.'" (Okay, pause. While we're at it, a sixty-five-year-old white man probably shouldn't use the word "fresh.") Poor Joe kept searching for a lifeline, telling Jon Stewart, "What I meant, was that he's got new ideas."

Then Stewart lowered his voice to a whisper, giving Biden some advice that would have been useful thirty years ago: "When you are about to say one of those things, take a deep breath and count to ten." The crowd laughed. Biden laughed.

There was one person, at least, who seemed unruffled by Biden's gaffe. "I didn't take Senator Biden's comments personally, but obviously they were historically inaccurate," said Barack Obama. "African American presidential candidates like Jesse Jackson, Shirley Chisholm, Carol Moseley Braun, and Al Sharpton gave a voice to many important issues through their campaigns, and no one would call them inarticulate."

Shake it off, Joe, shake it off. He pressed forward with the campaign. Maybe his luck would turn at the debates? But he started with a steep handicap, as the moderators gave Obama, Clinton, and Edwards the three plum positions on the stage and the bulk of the airtime.

Yet he found a way to make his presence felt. George Stephanopoulos asked the candidates to name the most dangerous country in the world.

"Iran," said Obama.

"Iran," said Clinton.

"Iran," said Edwards.

Then it was Biden's turn. "Pakistan."

The room did a double-take. *Wait, are you* allowed *to say Pakistan?* As Kaufman explains the logic, "Well, if Iran is a real problem because they *may* have nuclear weapons, Pakistan is a problem because they *already have* nuclear weapons." Plenty of national security experts agreed with him. (As recently as 2017, the former CIA station chief of Islamabad said, "With a failing economy, rampant terrorism, the fastest growing nuclear arsenal, the sixth largest population, and one of the highest birthrates in the world, Pakistan is of grave concern. . . . It probably is the most dangerous country for the world.")

"The guts it took to say that!" said Kaufman. "The safe thing to say was Iran . . . And anybody who was thinking said, 'You know, he's right about Pakistan.' And then they could tell that he was just saying what he believed." Whether you agreed with him or not about Pakistan, people noticed.

At least one person noticed: the junior senator from Illinois. "I absolutely think that the reason why Obama picked him for vice president was because of watching him on the Foreign Relations Committee, and going through the debates with him," suggests Kaufman. "This is a guy who is very, very knowledgeable and also self-confident, not in a bang-your-chest way, but self-confident in that he's willing to say what he believes in." It wasn't obvious at the time, but in a sense, Biden was rewarded for bucking the trend and just being himself.

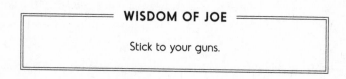

WISDOM OF JOE

Stick to your guns.

However, the average voter wasn't sussing out the dangers of Pakistan versus the dangers of Iran. The average voter knew only one thing about Biden: He said things like "clean" and "articulate" and seemed a bit gaffey. It even came up in the debates. Brian Williams gingerly raised the issue of those misfires, saying that "words have gotten you in trouble in the past." (*Brian Williams* said this. Pot? Meet kettle.) Williams asked Biden, given the famous loquaciousness, could he assure voters that he could control his mouth?

"Yes," said Biden.

A pause.

Yes, and . . . ?

That was it.

That was all Biden would say. He smiled. The crowd got the joke, laughed, and it might have been Biden's finest moment in either the '88 or '08 campaigns.

Biden couldn't nudge the polls, yet he stuck by his pledge to be "the best Biden I can be." He campaigned his way, the Joe Biden way, bluntly and unafraid to dive into the weeds of policy. The critics began to nod in approval. Biden is "giving Iowa voters full paragraphs of context instead of sound bites, making issues seem clear rather than simple," noted the *Philadelphia Inquirer*'s Thomas Fitzgerald. "He seems like a man liberated from the promise and tragedy of his past, serene in the shadows thrown by the star wattage of [Obama and Clinton]. . . . It's probably the last hurrah for his White House ambitions, and he's enjoying the ride."

And up until the Iowa caucuses, Biden still thought he had a puncher's chance. "My road to success is Iowa. It's the only playing field left out there," he reasoned. Maybe if he placed in the Top 3, he'd gain momentum and close the gap in New Hampshire.

Then came Iowa.

As we all know from the crack of lightning that changed the world, Obama won Iowa.

Then Edwards. Then Clinton.

Then . . . Bill Richardson.

Joe Biden's slice of the vote? One percent.

The night of that death-knell, he stayed upbeat and he addressed his supporters, including many who had been on Team Biden for decades. Jill. Val. "Look, folks, there's nothing to be sad about tonight," he told his crew, in a graceful withdrawal from the race. This is classic Joe. He had lost the election, yet *he* was the one cheering up the room.

Soon he would face the questions. Would he take a consolation prize, like maybe secretary of state?

"Absolutely, positively, unequivocally, Shermanesquely, no. I will not be anybody's secretary of state in any circumstance I can think of," Biden said.

Okay, got it. Well, how about vice president?

"And I absolutely can say, with certainty, I would not be anybody's vice president, period."

For sure?

"End of story. I guarantee I will not do it."

$=$

AS THE EPIC '08 PRIMARIES marched forward, Biden and Obama began to speak more often. "He'd call not so much to ask for advice as to bounce things off me," Biden said at the time.

"If you win, I'll do anything you ask me to," Biden said to Obama.

"Be careful, because I may ask you a lot," said Obama. "The only question I have is not whether I want you in this administration," Obama said, "it's which job you'd like best."

Meanwhile, the Obama brain trust chewed over the best choice for VP. Theoretically, you could pick someone to help you win a state—like how Kennedy used LBJ to flip Texas—but that's not what Obama had in mind. He had no appetite for electoral trickery. "I am more concerned and interested in how my selection may perform as an actual vice president than whether they will give a boost to the campaign," Obama said.

Obama's short list came down to three conventional white dudes: Evan Bayh, Tim Kaine, and Joe Biden. (Hillary Clinton was considered, but as has been widely reported, Obama worried that "Bill may be too big a complication. If I picked her, my concern is that there would be more than two of us in the relationship.") Evan Bayh and Tim Kaine were both safe, mainstream, unobjectionable choices, much like Diet Sprite. Yet they were not Joe Biden.

"We knew Biden could be somewhat long-winded and had a history of coloring outside the lines a bit," said Obama's campaign manager, David Plouffe, in an interview with Biden biographer Witcover. "But honestly, that was very appealing to Obama, because he wanted someone to give him the unvarnished truth. What do you need in a vice president? He knows and understands Congress, has great foreign policy and domestic experience. He had the whole package from a VP standpoint."

So in something of a secret meeting, Plouffe and top strategist

David Axelrod met Biden at Val's home. Before the Obama team could say anything, Biden started a "nearly twenty-minute monologue." As Plouffe remembers, Biden said, "I literally wouldn't have run if I knew the steamroller you guys would put together," and, "The last thing I should do is VP; after thirty-six years of being the top dog, it will be hard to be No. 2." Still talking and talking and talking, Biden said that he "would be a good soldier and could provide real value, domestically and internationally."

Plouffe wrote of that twenty-minute monologue, amused, "Ax and I couldn't get a word in edgewise." Yet he walked away satisfied, as he liked that while Biden "would accept the VP slot if offered, he was not pining for it." This trait had served Biden well before. Let's not forget that in 1972, before supporting Biden in his race for Senate, that Democratic bigwig had tested him, almost taunting him, wanting to see if Biden had a backbone. He did then. He did now.

So finally Obama and Biden had their tête-á-tête.

"Will this job be too small for you?" Obama asked.

"No, not as long as I would really be a confidant," Biden said. "The good news is, I'm sixty-five and you're not going to have to worry about my positioning myself to be president. The bad news is, I want to be part of the deal."

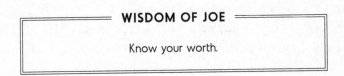

=== **WISDOM OF JOE** ===

Know your worth.

Biden had leverage. He was happy to walk away. If he wasn't VP? Then he'd be delighted to return to his old stomping grounds on the Foreign Relations Committee. By this point he had become, arguably, the most powerful force in the Senate. So like any good negotiator, he asked for a few additional conditions:

He wanted a weekly meeting with the president. *Done.*

He wanted a seat at the table. *Done.*

"One of the things I asked was, I said I don't want to be picked unless you're picking me for my judgment," Biden said later. "I said I want a commitment from you that in every important decision you'll make, every critical decision, economic and political as well as foreign policy, I'll get to be in the room."

Done.

BIDEN AND MUSCLE CARS

As Biden joined Team Obama, he would soon appear in an outlet even more prestigious than the *Times* or the *Post*: the pages of *The Onion*. "Taking advantage of the warm spring weather Monday, Vice President Joe Biden parked his 1981 Trans Am in the White House driveway, removed his undershirt, and spent a leisurely afternoon washing the muscle car and drinking beer," reports America's finest news source. An accompanying (fake) photo had Biden, bare-chested, wiping down his '81 beauty.

"'This baby just needs a little scrub down,'" he said in the satirical piece, "addressing a tour group as he tucked the sweat-covered top into the belt loop of his cutoff jean shorts. 'Gotta get her looking good so I can impress the chicks when I'm cruising down Pennsylvania [Avenue].'"

The Onion's piece might be an exaggeration, but it's only a *slight* distortion of Biden's lifelong passion for wheels. This is the son of Joe Sr., after all, who managed car dealerships in Delaware for thirty-four years. Hot Young Biden got to take them out for a spin, use them on dates, impress girls. For senior prom? He borrowed a 7,000-mile Chrysler 300D.

"I bought a '51 Studebaker," he told *Car and Driver*. "My dad thought it was nice and calm, but it had that overdrive, and it was fast. Then I bought a 1952 Plymouth convertible, candy-apple red with a split windshield. I think that was my favorite. I had a '56 Chevy, then in college I bought a 100,000-mile Mercedes 190SL with those Solex carburetors that never functioned. And I still have my 1967 Goodwood-green Corvette, 327, 350-horse, with a rear-axle ratio that really gets up and goes. The Secret Service won't let me drive it. I'm not allowed to drive anything. It's the one thing I hate about this job. I'm serious."

Oh, and about *The Onion*'s caricature? Biden called them out. "You think I'd drive a Trans Am?" he said, laughing. "I have been in my bathing suit in my driveway and not only washed my Goodwood-green 1967 Corvette but also simonized it. At least *The Onion* should have had me washing a Trans Am convertible. I love convertibles."

And once again, the humor cloaks a deeper pathos. "My fondest memory of that Corvette," he told *Popular Mechanics*, is when Hunter was three years old. "[He was] sitting on my lap while I was driving—I know it's bizarre now to say that. We lived out in a rural area, and we came to a stop sign on a country road. A beautiful day like today, and he's sitting on my lap, and he turns around and puts his hand on my face and he says, 'Daddy? Daddy? I love you more than the whole sky.'"

On August 23, 2008, in Springfield, Illinois, Obama and Biden appeared together as a team, as buddies, for the very first time. Biden seemed reborn. Rejuvenated. Grinning and pointing and doing Biden-y things. Obama was fired up and ready to go, making the case for why Biden was the perfect choice for VP:

Biden has "brought change to Washington, but Washington hasn't changed him."

Accurate.

"He's an expert on foreign policy whose heart and values are firmly rooted in the middle class."

Yep.

"He is uniquely suited to be my partner."

Yep, that too, more than he would know.

Soon Joe would be introduced, in Denver, at the Democratic National Convention. With his thirty-six years of experience in the Senate—and with that Rolodex of world leaders—he could have asked anyone to give his introduction. Who would he pick? A presidential heavyweight, like Bill Clinton? A senatorial comrade, like John Kerry?

He chose the man he respected more than anyone in the world. He chose someone who had been at his side since the 1960s.

He chose his son. Beau Biden.

"I know [Joe] as an incredible father and a loving grandfather," Beau began. He had his father's jaw and those earnest eyes. The Denver crowd was mesmerized. "A man who hustled home to Delaware after the last vote so he wouldn't miss me and my brother's games. Who, after returning from some war-torn region of the world, would tiptoe into our room and kiss us good night. Who turns down some fancy cocktail party in Washington so he won't miss my daughter, Natalie's, birthday party."

And in just a few captivating minutes, with his father looking on, tears welling, Beau gave us all a hint of what makes Joe Biden such an endearing figure.

"Now, some people poke fun at my dad talking too much," Beau said as the crowd chuckled. "What a lot of people don't know is that, when he was young, he had a severe stutter. The kids called him Dash—not because he was fast on the football field, which he was, but like a dash at the end of a sentence you can't finish. But now he speaks with a clear and strong voice. He says what needs to be said. And he does what needs to be done."

Jill looked on, fighting back emotion. Michelle Obama wiped her eyes.

Beau mentioned that "because of other duties, it won't be possible for me to be here this fall to stand by him the way he stood by me," leaving unspoken that his "other duties" were to serve the country in Iraq—he had volunteered for the National Guard. He finished up: "So I have something to ask of you. Be there for my dad like he was for me. Please join me in welcoming my friend, my father, my hero, and the next vice president of the United States: Joe Biden."

He and Beau shared a tight, fierce hug that lasted for several seconds. Beau gave his father a kiss on the cheek. Behind them was a backdrop of red signs: BIDEN! BIDEN! BIDEN!

Many of us can remember watching this speech in 2008, but at the time we didn't *really* know Joe Biden. We didn't know about his loss. And none of us, of course, could know the tragedy that loomed ahead. Now we do. Looking back, these words have newfound weight. Joe looked at his son. "Beau, I love you. I am so proud of you. Proud of the son you are. Proud of the father you've become. . . . And I'm so proud of my son Hunter, my daughter, Ashley, and my wife, Jill, the only one who leaves me breathless and speechless at the same time."

Biden introduced America to his mother, Jean, ninety-one years young, the one who had the guts to challenge the nuns, and the one who told him: "Nobody is better than you. You're not better than anybody else, but *nobody* is any better than you."

Then he told us what his father had told him, all those many years ago: "Champ, when you're knocked down, get up! Get up!"

PART III

THE VEEP

8

From Gaffes to Glory (2008—2016)

*"The number one issue facing the
middle class [is] a three-letter word: Jobs.
J-O-B-S."*

JOE.

JOE.

How many times did Barack Obama say that to himself?

At times, the gaffes seemed endless. On the campaign trail, Biden reminded us that "when the stock market crashed, Franklin Roosevelt got on the television," yet the stock market crashed in 1929, or about three years before FDR became president.

Then he gave an omen: "Mark my words. It will not be six months before the world tests Barack Obama like they did John Kennedy. Watch, we're going to have an international crisis, a generated crisis to test the mettle of this guy." Republicans smacked their lips, weaponizing this line against Obama.

In a classic moment of Biden-y bluntness, he said that Hillary Clinton was "as qualified or more qualified than I am to be vice president of America, and quite frankly, it might have been a better pick." Okay,

Joe. And Republicans gleefully pounced on a careless comment from earlier in the election, when he said that "you cannot go to a 7-Eleven or a Dunkin' Donuts unless you have a slight Indian accent." He was trying to make the point that the demographics had changed and there was now a larger Indian population in Delaware, but still. *Joe.*

But wait, there's more! At a campaign rally, feeding off the energy of the room, Biden raised his voice, joyful, and urged a man named Chuck Graham, a state senator, to stand up and show himself to the crowd. "Stand up, Chuck! Let 'em see ya! Stand up, Chuck!"

Only one hiccup.

Chuck was in a wheelchair.

"Oh, God love ya, what am I talking about?" Biden said, scrambling to recover. "I tell you what, you're making everyone else stand up though, pal. Thank you very, very much." He turned back to the crowd. "I tell you what, stand up for Chuck!" The crowd stood, cheered, clapped, and Biden left the podium to go meet Chuck and shake his hand, smiling. "You can tell I'm new."

Thanks to goofs like this, reports later surfaced of friction between Obama and his No. 2. At one point "a chill set in between [Obama headquarters] and the Biden plane," according to John Heilemann and Mark Halperin, authors of *Game Change*, and "Joe and Obama barely spoke by phone, barely campaigned together." They report that Obama became "increasingly frustrated with his running mate after Biden let loose with a string of gaffes," and when Biden "made the prediction that Obama would be tested with an international crisis, the Illinois senator had had enough. 'How many times is Biden gonna say something stupid?' he demanded of his advisers on a conference call."

Yet even on the bumpy road of the campaign, Biden started to put these miscues behind him and show Team Obama, as he said years ago, "the essence of Joe Biden." Videographer Arun Chaudhary's team was split in two—most on Obama's plane, then some on Biden's. "At first, people would complain when they had to do Biden duty, because it felt like you were getting kicked off the grown-up plane and put on the junior plane," says Chaudhary. "And then, one by one, Joe Biden just won them over. Every one of them would come back to me with some story like, 'It was late at night, and we were just talking, and he wanted to know about my family, and he had really good questions.' All of a sudden, the prized job was to be on the Biden plane."

The team soon found that the Biden energy was nonstop. At a random hotel in Ohio, to blow off some steam, Herbie Ziskend hit the gym and did some abs work. He then saw this guy in the corner going full-speed, hyperintense, wearing a ball cap. *Is that Joe frickin' Biden?* "He's doing endless pushups and biceps curls," says Ziskend. "He's obviously working harder than anybody. And he's forty-five years older than me."

Sometimes the best Biden moments are the small ones, the tiny gestures, the lift of an eyebrow or the squeeze of a bicep. Chaudhary remembers following both Obama and Biden to a biodiesel factory that takes chicken waste and converts it into energy. Obama, true to form, made some comments about the importance of biodiesel fuel and how it relates to energy policy. Biden? "He just kept holding up vials of liquid and saying, 'Chicken manure,' in this really satisfied tone of voice," says Chaudhary. You can visualize the solemn nod, the squinted eyes, the hint of a smile. *Chicken manure. Heh.*

Given the backdrop of all the prior gaffes, Biden probably doesn't get enough credit for the trickiest job he had in the 2008 campaign: the debate against Sarah Palin. This could have so easily gone sideways. Biden had thirty-six years of senatorial experience, he had met every world leader, and, boy, did he love telling you how much he knew. Sarah Palin, well, was Sarah Palin. If Biden said *anything* that could be perceived as belittling, condescending, sexist, or mansplaining, then suddenly Palin would emerge with a bounce, and God knows how that might wound the campaign.

He took the debate seriously. Unlike that fateful debate in '87 where he winged it and flubbed the Neil Kinnock quote, this time he knuckled down. Practiced. And when he finished his prep sessions, the last two people in the room were his sons, Hunter and Beau. He had always given them that privilege to ease their minds: *wild card*. Now they had the chance to return the favor. To comfort him and to give him calm, Beau looked at Joe and said, "Look at me, Dad. Look at me. Remember, remember home base. Remember."

=== **WISDOM OF JOE** ===

Remember home base.

Biden remembered. Against Palin he struck just the right note of competence, statesmanship, and humility. *Saturday Night Live* had a field day with what Biden presumably *wanted* to say. "My goal tonight was a simple one," said *SNL*-Biden, as played by Jason Sudeikis. "To come up here, and at no point seem like a condescending, egomaniacal bully. And I'm gonna be honest, I think I nailed it. Sure, there are moments when I wanted to say, *Hey, this lady's a dummy!*, but I didn't. Because Joe Biden is better than that. I repeat. Joe Biden is *better* than that." *SNL* took one more swing that's worth revisiting. You know how Biden always talks about his working-class roots of Scranton? *SNL*-Biden takes it up a notch: "I come from Scranton, Pennsylvania. And that's as hardscrabbled a place as you're going to find. I'll show you around sometime, and you'll see. It's a hellhole! An absolute jerk-water of a town ... It's just an awful, awful sad place. So don't be telling me that I'm part of the Washington elite, because I come from the absolute worst place on earth, Scranton, Pennsylvania," He flashes a Biden-smile. "And Wilmington, Delaware's, not much better."

=====

BOOSTED, AT LEAST IN PART, by Biden's strong performance, Obama won both the electoral college (365–173) and the popular vote, which is something that used to happen in American history. And in January of 2009, Joe Biden took two different Oaths of Office. One was for VP, the other for senator. In what must have been a bittersweet departure, after thirty-six years of fighting for his beloved Delaware constituents, he had won his old Senate seat for the seventh—*seventh!*—straight time. (Biden's vacant seat would be filled by the guy who had supported him, faithfully, since that very first Hail Mary in '72: Ted Kaufman.) After officially becoming the United States' forty-seventh vice president, Biden joined in the celebratory parade, did a little jog, and smiled as well-wishers shouted "Joe! Joe! Joe!" The Secret Service gave him a code name: Celtic.

Biden immediately made himself useful, helping to persuade Hillary Clinton to accept secretary of state. (The two were close from their years in the Senate, and on the phone he'd tell her, "I love you, darling." Before you think that he's flirting, remember that Joe Biden loves everyone.)

And if people thought that Joe Biden was going to keep his mouth shut when he became vice president, people didn't know Joe Biden. He kept saying what he saw as the God's honest truth ... even when it hurt him. In the early days he acknowledged that "If we do everything right, if we do it with absolute certainty, if we stand up there and we really make the tough decisions, there's still a thirty percent chance we're going to get it wrong."

The press drooled over this one: *30 percent chance you're going to get it wrong? And get* what *wrong, precisely?*

At Obama's very first prime-time press briefing (remember those?), he was asked about this mysterious 30 percent. "What were you talking about?" the reporter asked. "In general [do] you agree with that ratio of success, 30 percent failure, 70 percent success?"

Obama laughed. "You know, I don't remember exactly what Joe was referring to, not surprisingly."

The reporters chuckled.

"But let me try this out." Obama then gave a lengthy, measured response about how their decisions might have uncertain consequences, and how the country needed a recovery package, and yada yada yada; then he admitted, finally, "I have no idea. I really don't."

Wait, did Obama just throw some shade at Biden? That's sure what it sounded like to Maureen Dowd, who wrote, "Joe is nothing if not loyal. And the president should return that quality, and not leave his lieutenant vulnerable to *Odd Couple* parodies."

"Biden felt insulted," reported *Newsweek*. "Through staffers, Obama apologized, protesting that he had meant no disrespect. But at one of their regularly scheduled weekly lunches, Biden directly raised the incident with the president. The veep said he was trying to be more disciplined about his own remarks, but he asked in return that the president refrain from making fun (and require his staff to do likewise). He made the point that even the impression that the president was dissing him was not only bad for Biden, but bad for the administration. The conversation cleared the air."

Given the deep friendship we now associate with Biden and Obama, this feels like ancient history, but it's sneakily instructive. Those early hiccups suggest that the Obama/Biden friendship was not inevitable, it was not always easy, and sometimes it wobbled. All relationships, even bromances, take work.

Before Biden had time to truly settle into his new residence at the Naval Observatory, Team Obama was tossed another curveball: swine flu. As the nation started to panic, Biden said on *Today*, "I would tell members of my family—and I have—I wouldn't go anywhere in confined places now." More panic. The travel industry blew a gasket. Once again Biden had gone off-script. Later that evening, Biden ran into Ziskend and threw an arm around him, staying upbeat, boosting morale. "Are we winning today?" he asked with that smile of his.

"I don't know about today, sir," Ziskend said a bit nervously.

A beat. "You're right, we're not," Biden said.

It lightened the mood and gave Ziskend some perspective. "He was being funny, but he was also showing me that, well, he had had *many* days," Ziskend says now. "He'd been doing this for thirty-six years. It's a lesson to all the people who were running around like headless chickens—this is *one* day, and there were going to be many, many more days. When you've seen enough of these cycles, you know how it goes." This type of mind-set, and a focus on the longer arc, is what helps Biden avoid getting flustered by minor gaffes, and pivot to the important work that lies ahead.

WISDOM OF JOE

There will be many more days.

Meanwhile, Biden had to figure out the answer to a very simple question: What does a vice president *do*, exactly? If you ask John Adams, it's the "most insignificant office that ever the invention of man contrived." In LBJ's opinion, the office isn't "worth a warm bucket of piss." And if you're Aaron Burr, well, maybe you shoot someone in a duel.

Biden understood that because the Constitution failed to provide a VP instruction manual, he would need to study the people who had come before him, analyze what worked and what didn't, and then choose a model to follow. To help with his due diligence, he met in person with not just the Democrats (Al Gore and Walter Mondale), but also Dick Cheney and George H. W. Bush. He thought about the various VP archetypes:

DICK CHENEY: Biden considered him the most dangerous veep in the nation's history, and on the campaign he had vowed to "restore the balance" of the vice president. Perhaps he met with Cheney to figure out what *not* to do, or as a courtesy, but this was (clearly) not his model.

DAN QUAYLE: Biden viewed Quayle as strictly an ideologue, and therefore not the right model. That said . . . "My favorite vice president is Dan Quayle," Biden later said to his sister, Val. This threw her. *Um, why?* Because Quayle had installed a pool at the VP's residence, and now Biden's grandkids could use it to go swimming, and he could run around with squirt guns.

AL GORE: Gore tended to focus on a few key areas— government reorganization, technology, and obviously the environment. Biden was tempted by this, but he was concerned about getting stuck in just one or two boxes, unable to see the full picture.

WALTER MONDALE: Mondale was perhaps the dark horse, but Biden found him appealing. He thought about the historical parallels to Jimmy Carter, who came into office young, inexperienced, and with a veteran veep. Back in the '70s, Mondale had written Carter a memo outlining how he could function as something of a general advisor, a do-it-all trusted confidant. "Mondale gave Biden a copy of the memo, and they met three times," explains Witcover. "Biden, who thought similarly, concluded that this model was better suited to Obama's needs and his own desires and skills. With Obama's full agreement, Biden proceeded to organize his own vice presidency accordingly."

From the jump, Biden thought of himself as the advisor-in-chief. "Every single solitary appointment he has made thus far, I have been in the room," he said in December 2008. "The recommendations I have made in most cases, coincidentally, have been the recommendations that he's picked. Not because I made them, but because we think a lot alike." Biden quickly became a steady hand, a go-to guy whom Obama could dispatch to solve seemingly any problem: *Joe, you do Iraq. Joe, you do the debt ceiling. Joe, you do the Stimulus tracking.* The gaffes would melt into the background. Despite the caricatures, he would not be Uncle Joe, and while a few lovable, shoot-from-the-hip moments of candor would still bubble to the surface, they would not define his vice presidency. Instead he played many roles, and he played them well. Let's look at each.

JOE THE AMBASSADOR

This role was a natural fit. Obama would send Biden to crisscross the globe, leveraging all those years on the world stage. Take Jerusalem. In 2010, Biden flew to Israel to give a speech in which he promised "absolute, total, unvarnished commitment to Israeli security." So far so good! Then things got awkward when Israel announced—while Biden was there—that they would build 1,600 new settlements.

Shit. How to play this? He didn't mince words (he never does). In public he blasted the move, charging that it "undermines the trust we need right now." Then he took it up a notch. He and Jill were scheduled to have a double dinner-date with Benjamin "Bibi" Netanyahu and his wife, Sara. Biden showed up late, sending a clear signal.

He later pulled Netanyahu aside, and to underscore the point that Bibi should take a bigger step for peace—nothing small would do—he told the Israeli prime minister some old advice from his father: "There's no sense dying on a small cross." Was there awkward silence? A glare? As one pundit said, "Few American politicians would think it wise to invoke crucifixion in a conversation with the leader of the Jewish state," but after Biden's folksy dollop of wisdom ... Netanyahu just laughed. "I have to tell you," an Israeli ambassador said at the time, "it is the single most succinct understanding of Israeli political reality of any other statement that I've heard."

Herbie Ziskend was there for this now-legendary interaction. "He had known Netanyahu for decades. I don't know how that scenario would have played out if he had been, like, a one-term governor and had never met Netanyahu," says Ziskend. "But it was like two old friends reconnecting. Again, it speaks to just the importance of those long-term relationships."

Biden's secret to diplomacy? It comes down to authenticity, which sometimes requires you to go off-script, to ditch the canned rhetoric. Biden would roll his eyes at the "official" talking points. "They'll give me a line and I'll say, 'I'm not gonna say that! That's simply not believable!'" he said in 2014. "It's really very important, if you are able, to communicate to the other guy that you understand his problem. And some of this diplomatic bullshit communicates, 'We have no idea of your problem.'"

Thanks to all of Biden's strong relationships, he would soon be tapped for missions in Ukraine, Japan, Korea, Colombia. "This personal element is, perhaps, why Biden is regularly handed the lemons in the foreign-policy sphere—the tough, unglamorous cases, the ones that have to be worked for a long time," suggests *The Atlantic*'s Steve Clemons. "There are leaders Obama never really warmed up to. Biden tends these relationships."

And as we saw with Milošević, the war criminal, sometimes diplomacy takes some tough love. In 2011, Biden met with Vladimir Putin in his Kremlin office. Putin, proud of the handsome furniture and decorations, turned to Biden and said through an interpreter, "It's amazing what capitalism will do, won't it? A magnificent office!"

Biden moved close to Vlad, close, closer, closer—so close that the two men could almost kiss—and said, "Mr. Prime Minister, I'm looking into your eyes, and I don't think you have a soul."

Putin looked back at him. Smiled. "We understand one another."

JOE THE POT-STIRRER

Biden likes to ask the tough questions. Challenge assumptions. So when Obama was faced with the most agonizing choices of his presidency— like whether to boost the number of troops in Afghanistan—Biden unleashed his inner interrogator, just like he did when chairing the Bork proceedings.

Quick recap: As the war in Afghanistan slid into mayhem, the generals requested 50,000 more troops. Obama refused to make a snap decision. (Too many wars, in Obama's mind, were launched by snap decisions.) So the president demanded more data, more options, more intel, determined to undergo a rigorous review. Obama and the generals had meeting after meeting.

Biden was the chief skeptic, pressing the generals and pushing for clarity.

"In the midst of that debate, Joe and I would have lengthy one-on-one conversations, trying to tease out what, precisely, are our interests in Afghanistan, what exactly can we achieve there," Obama explained to *The New Yorker*'s Evan Osnos. "There were times where Joe would ask questions, essentially on my behalf, to give me decision-making space, to help stir up a vigorous debate."

In one meeting in the Situation Room, as *Newsweek* reported, Biden interjected with a question. "Can I just clarify a factual point? How much will we spend this year on Afghanistan?"

$65 billion.

"And how much will we spend on Pakistan?"

$2.25 billion.

"Well, by my calculations that's a thirty-to-one ratio in favor of Afghanistan," Biden continued. "So I have a question. Al Qaeda is almost all in Pakistan, and Pakistan has nuclear weapons. And yet for every dollar we're spending in Pakistan, we're spending thirty dollars in Afghanistan. Does that make strategic sense?"

Silence. "But the questions had their desired effect," reported *Newsweek*'s Holly Bailey. "Those gathered began putting more thought into Pakistan as the key theater in the region."

Afghanistan, Pakistan, Iraq, health care, budget reconciliation deals—Biden was always there, always stirring the pot. "Joe is very good about sometimes articulating what's on other people's minds, or things that they've said in private conversations that people have been less willing to say in public," said Obama. "Joe's not afraid to tell me what he thinks. And that's exactly what I need, and exactly what I want."

WISDOM OF JOE

Have the guts to ask the tough questions.

And let's not forget another pot that he stirred. On May 6, 2012, on *Meet the Press*, David Gregory asked Biden if his views on gay marriage had evolved.

Biden spoke slowly, quietly, earnestly. "This is all about . . . a simple proposition," he said, hands clasped. "Who do you love? *Who do you love*, and will you be loyal to the person you love? And that's what people are finding out is what all marriages at their root are about. Whether they are marriages of lesbians or gay men or heterosexuals."

Gregory wanted to clarify. "And you're comfortable with same-sex marriage now?"

"I am absolutely comfortable with the fact that men marrying men, women marrying women, and heterosexual men and women marrying one another, are entitled to the same exact rights," Biden said. "All the civil rights, all the civil liberties. And quite frankly, I don't see much of a distinction beyond that."

Whether he had intended to or not, Joe Biden had just made history, and we all know what happened next. This is "accidental wisdom" at its finest.

BIDEN AND MEMES

Historians can debate whether Joe Biden is the greatest or most influential vice president ever, but there is no question he is the meme-iest VP in American history.

Some highlights:

JOE: I hid all the pens from Trump.
OBAMA: Why?
JOE: Because he bringing his own.
OBAMA: ???
JOE: HE'S BRINGING HIS OWN PENCE.

JOE: I'm going to ask Donald if he wants something to eat.
BARACK: That's nice, Joe.
JOE: And then I'm going to offer him knuckle sandwiches.

OBAMA: Any good ideas on how to defeat ISIS?
Biden raises hand
OBAMA: Besides assembling the Avengers?
Biden lowers hand

Before Trump's inauguration, one meme had Obama on the phone with a caption: "I know Joe called and ordered 500 pizzas to be delivered on January 21st, but I need you to cancel that order."

Or another, with a pic of the two of them grinning, partners in crime:

BIDEN: C'mon you gotta print a fake birth certificate, put it in an envelope labeled "SECRET," and leave it in the oval office desk.
OBAMA: Joe.

Biden has seen the memes, and he likes them. When his daughter, Ashley, introduced him to the bromance memes, she says that "he sat there for an hour and laughed." He even has a favorite. A photo shows Obama and Joe in an embrace, about to hug, and looking into each other's eyes:

"See? Doesn't this feel right?"
"Joe I'm not leaving my wife for you."
"You said we'd be together forev—"
"8 years. I said 8 years."

JOE THE DEAL-MAKER

In 2009, the Democrats controlled fifty-nine seats in the Senate. That wasn't enough to muscle through the Affordable Care Act, where they would need sixty to break a filibuster.

Yet they had a surprising card to play. Senator Arlen Specter, from Pennsylvania, had been a Republican since 1965. Yet guess who he knew from years of commuting on the Amtrak? He and Biden were close. When Joe sensed that his friend was wavering, he met with Specter six times in person and called him an additional eight times, urging him to switch teams and join the Democrats. The courtship paid off. (Quick refresher: Back in 1991, then-Republican Arlen Specter had a cameo in the Clarence Thomas hearings, acting as

Anita Hill's interrogator. Biden knows that yesterday's opponent can be today's ally. . . .)

When Specter hopped across the aisle, the Democrats now had exactly sixty senators. Without Biden's charm campaign, would the ACA have passed? Obviously the future of health care will be debated for years and decades, but the one thing we know is that, as Biden said the day it passed—while miked-up for all the world to hear—"This is a big fucking deal."

And when Republicans threatened to not raise the debt ceiling, which suddenly risked an economic meltdown, Biden got on the phone with his old frenemy Mitch McConnell. As a Reuters headline put it, Biden was seen as the "last hope" for the negotiations. He huddled up with a gang of his old colleagues, Democrats and Republicans. A deal didn't happen overnight. Some Republicans left the table, then came back. They had a second session, a third session. The nightmare stretched for months. And when a compromise was finally secured, Obama and John Boehner would announce the deal and get all the credit, but "it was Biden's close working relationship with McConnell that broke the months-long logjam," according to Politico.

As McConnell later said, "We got results that would not have been possible without a negotiating partner like Joe Biden. Obviously, I don't always agree with him, but I do trust him." This might be why Biden has another nickname: "The McConnell Whisperer."

JOE THE COMEDIAN

The Gridiron Club is one of the oldest organizations of journalists. Every year, the president is invited to a comedy roast of the Who's Who in media—basically a JV version of the White House Correspondents'

Dinner. Politicians are expected to tell jokes. One year Obama played hooky at Camp David, and asked Biden to pinch-hit.

Biden's eyes must have gone wide. *Finally* he gets to say whatever the hell he wants, with no penalty! It's *supposed* to be funny! Some of his stand-up bits:

- "Axelrod really wanted me to do this on teleprompter, but I told him I'm much better when I wing it," he began. "I know these evenings run long, so I'm going to be brief—talk about the audacity of hope."
- "President Obama does send his greetings, though. He can't be here tonight because he's busy getting ready for Easter. He thinks it's about him."
- "I understand these are dark days for the newspaper business, but I hate it when people say newspapers are obsolete. That's totally untrue. I know from firsthand experience. I recently got a puppy, and you can't housebreak a puppy on the Internet."
- "I never realized just how much power Dick Cheney had, until my first day on the job. I walked into my office . . . I opened my drawer, and Dick Cheney had left me Barack Obama's birth certificate!"

This was Biden *trying* to be funny. As we all know, he does his best work when the comedy is unintentional. Like when he visited Harvard and met the vice president of the student body, and said off the cuff, grinning, "Isn't it a bitch, this vice president thing?"

Or the time when he introduced an elderly couple, commenting, "There's an old Irish saying, that says, may the hinges of your friendship never go rusty." Biden said to the crowd, "Well, with these two folks, there's no doubt about them staying oiled and lubricated." He heard the crowd laugh and groan, and then cracked a large grin, suddenly realizing what he had just implied. "Now, for you who are not Irish . . . 'lubricated' has a different meaning for us Irish."

Biden seemed to have a special fondness for Irish gaffes. Take the time he introduced the prime minister of Ireland. Likely thrilled to get back in touch with his Celtic roots, Biden told reporters, with the prime minister right beside him, "His mom lived in Long Island for ten years or so. God rest her soul."

Biden then paused, thought for a quick second. "Although, she's—wait—your mom's still alive. It was your dad [who] passed."

Ireland's PM awkwardly nodded.

Biden didn't miss a beat. "God bless her soul!" he said, laughing, and the prime minister laughed, too.

JOE THE RAINMAKER

In February of 2009, Congress passed the $787 billion stimulus package to help rescue the economy from the maw of depression. That was the headline. But what happened next? Where did the money go? Who kept track of it?

Joe Biden kept track of it.

Obama gave Biden the sprawling job of overseeing the project. As Biden says, it's "the largest economic stimulus in history, larger than the entire New Deal." $30 billion to health information technology. $48 billion to transportation projects. $90 billion into renewable power and advanced biofuels. (Those vials of liquids from the factory again. *Biofuels. Chicken manure. Heh.*)

Like he does with everything, he obsessed over the details until he became a wonk. In June of 2010, for example, Biden joined Mayor Bloomberg at the Brooklyn Bridge, where funds had been allocated for repairs and upgrades. It was a fairly innocent event—just a quick speech about how the stimulus bill was helping to fund roads and tunnels and bridges. Nothing too complicated.

"But then he started drilling me on the components of every piece of spending," remembers Ziskend. "And he had this *deep* understanding of the most efficient way that federal dollars can go into bridges and tunnels and roads, and he starts just asking me every piece of it. And it was amazing."

JOE THE HUGGER

In 2009, Biden took trip after trip to Iraq and Afghanistan. He needed to. Obama had asked him to give a no-bullshit assessment of the facts on the ground, good or bad. Biden would meet with the troops, give them pep talks. ("As corny as it sounds, *damn*, I'm proud to be an American," he said to one crew.) On one of these trips, Biden met with a unit of soldiers that happened to have a certain captain in their ranks—a man who had volunteered for National Guard duty . . . Captain Beau Biden, wearing his desert fatigues. Father and son had an emotional hug.

Then Biden hit the cafeteria to mix it up with the soldiers. "He lit up like a 1,000-watt bulb," reported the *New York Times*'s James Traub. "Biden shook every hand, and threw his arm around every shoulder—hundreds and hundreds of them. 'How are you, man?' he cried, with fresh joy, to each table of soldiers. 'Did you get a picture of me?' A soldier said politely, 'Look this way, sir,' and Biden, who has the blinding white teeth of a starlet, whirled around with a huge smile. The vice president never stopped moving, smiling, or talking."

Biden has always been a hugger, regardless of whether his victims are men, women, kids, grandpas, family, strangers. Take the swearing-in ceremonies of new senators (in both 2013 and 2015), which were caught on C-SPAN, and which have become something of a Biden cult classic. "You've got beautiful eyes, Mom, holy mackerel!" he said to one old lady. He mugged for selfies. Touched another old lady's cheek. Rubbed shoulders. He appraised one couple and said, "You married up, son." To a muscular guy he said, "Call me if you need help on your pecs."

JOE (AND JILL) THE PRANKSTERS

The Internet fell in love with the idea of Joe the Prankster. And there might be some truth to this. Biden would hide M&Ms throughout the White House, as something of a gentle ribbing to Michelle Obama's healthy eating campaign. And it's *definitely* true that Biden is a prankster . . .

. . . Jill Biden.

She took pride in her nickname of "Captain of the Vice Squad," and she earned that title with stunt after stunt, such as the one Valentine's Day when she snuck into Joe's office to use a stick of lipstick to graffiti the windows with "Jill loves Joe" and "Happy [Heart] Valentine's Day." And if this strikes you as treacly, you'll be happy to know that on Halloween, she once surprised Joe by placing a fake rat on his podium.

One morning after getting up early, while Joe was still in bed, she raced into the room to wake him up. "Joe, don't you have a breakfast this morning? People are coming through the gate!"

He threw off the covers, panicked, and said, "I do, I do!"

"April Fool's!" Jill yelled out.

She has been known to wear disguises, like the time she pretended to be a server at a party she hosted. She has worn red wigs.

Yet nothing will top the time that Joe, on Air Force Two, reached up to open the overhead compartment, ready to stow his luggage.

Boo!

Jill had climbed into the overheard compartment, just to surprise him.

But just like her husband, beneath the pranks and the jokes is a person of rock-solid values, hard work, and a lifelong devotion to public service—in her case, through teaching. She taught English at community colleges for decades, earned her doctoral degree at the University of Delaware, and then Dr. Jill Biden became, as Obama put it, "the first Second Lady in our nation's history to keep her day job," as she kept teaching classes. She wrote a children's book titled *Don't Forget, God Bless Our Troops*, inspired by Beau's deployment in Iraq, and how that affected his daughter. Along with Michelle Obama she cofounded Joining Forces, which supports veterans and military families, and she also found time to launch the Biden Breast Health Initiative.

So it's easy to understand why Joe sometimes introduces himself as "Jill's husband." Although other times he's less smooth, like when he gave a speech praising the nation's teachers, calling them "the best-kept secret in America," and then said, "I think I'd have the same attitude [even if] I did not sleep with a community college professor every night." The crowd laughed. Biden quickly clarified. "Oh, the same one, the same one!"

We all know that oldest of clichés, "Love takes work," and perhaps that's true, but sometimes it just takes a damn good laugh.

JOE THE COOL BOSS

In January of 2009, on his very first team meeting, Biden told his staff something that they didn't expect to hear. They had likely envisioned a talk about the importance of the job, the long hours they would need to work, or the sacrifices that they would make. And of course they would indeed work long hours and sacrifice, but that was not Biden's message.

"The absolute most important thing is your family," Biden told his staff, as Ziskend remembers. "Make sure that's all taken care of. I don't want to hear that you're putting off going to a Little League game, or that you're straining your relationships because you're not seeing your loved one."

Ziskend couldn't believe it. "This was our *first* staff meeting. He really set the example." And Biden stuck by that principle. Years later, in 2014, he sent a memo to his staff on work-life balance. It's worth printing in full:

To My Wonderful Staff,

I would like to take a moment and make something clear to everyone. I do not expect, nor do I want, any of you to miss or sacrifice important family obligations for work. Family obligations include, but are not limited to, family birthdays, anniversaries, weddings, any religious ceremonies, such as first communions and bar mitzvahs, graduations, and times of need, such as an illness or a loss in the family. This is very important to me. In fact, I will go so far as to say that if I find out that you are working with me while missing important family responsibilities, it will disappoint me greatly. This has been an unwritten rule since my days in the Senate.

Thank you all for the hard work.

> *Sincerely,*
> *Joe*

The staff was touched. The world was touched. And when we know Joe Biden's full story—especially the story of what would happen just a year later, with Beau—we know that when it comes to family, he means every damn one of these words. By nearly any conceivable standard, Biden's run as VP had been a success. He had racked up the wins. Yet no matter how well things are going in your career, as Biden once said, "Reality has a way of intruding."

Reality intruded in 1972. Reality would intrude once more.

9

Beau (1969—2015)

"A parent knows success when his child turns out better than he did.
In the words of the Biden family:
Beau Biden was, quite simply, the finest man any of us have ever known."

NOTHING ABOUT THIS CHAPTER IN Biden's life feels fair. How could one man survive so much tragedy?

Ever since the accident of 1972, Biden had a close relationship with his two sons. He knew it, too. "The incredible bond I have with my children is the gift I'm not sure I would have had, had I not been through what I went through," he said in 2015.

That bond seemed especially strong with his elder son.

Beau's life, his values, and his choices help us gain an even richer understanding of Joe. The similarities between the two are striking. Joe went to the Catholic Archmere Academy. Beau went to the Catholic Archmere Academy. Joe went to Syracuse Law School, inspired by Neilia. So did Beau. Joe devoted his life to public service. Beau devoted his life to public service, serving as Delaware's attorney general.

When we peel one level deeper, the parallels are even more revealing. Joe worked to end the genocide in Bosnia. In 1998, after the war had ravaged Kosovo, as a private lawyer, Beau traveled to the region, where he helped train local judges and prosecutors. (Kosovo would later name a highway in Beau's honor, marking "a symbol of the enduring friendship between Kosovo and the United States.") Beau had his father's eloquence, his earnest charisma, and even his jawline. As Obama said, "He even looked and sounded like Joe, although I think Joe would be first to acknowledge that Beau was an upgrade—Joe 2.0."

Joe has a go-to saying: *I give you my word as a Biden.* Beau internalized the lesson; his life is filled with story after story of personal integrity. Consider: When Joe visited Beau's National Guard's unit in Iraq, Stephen Colbert offered to film a segment of a father-and-son reunion. Beau nixed the idea—he didn't want the free publicity, and why should he be treated differently from his fellow soldiers? At the time he was Delaware's attorney general, and clearly that segment would have been good for "optics." Beau wasn't an optics guy. ("He didn't want any special attention," remembered Colbert. "He didn't want to leave his unit. He didn't want to be singled out.")

Beau did things the hard way, the right way. At first, Delaware's governor offered to appoint Beau to be the attorney general, filling a vacancy. He turned it down so that, as Obama said, he could run in an election and "win it fair and square." (After Beau won the election, one local paper ran with the headline "Biden Most Popular Man in Delaware—Beau.") He then poured his energy into punishing the worst of the worst—sex offenders. Biden's father had a saying: *It takes a small man to hit a small child.* Beau had learned from the elder Bidens, and just like his father, Joe, he looked out for the little guy.

Beau did this in college, too. When speaking to students at Syracuse, Joe Biden told a story about courage, about what it means to be a man, and about his son Beau. The story was about sexual assault on campus. First he acknowledged something that we never talk about:

For most guys, if we spot trouble with the way a man is treating a woman, it can be hard to speak up. *It's none of my business,* we're tempted to think. "It's hard. It's a hard thing for a guy on campus to step in," Joe acknowledged.

"My son stepped in," Joe told the crowd of college students, speaking in a slow, level, deadly serious voice that had no trace of Uncle Joe. "He stepped in when a guy was mauling a coed in a coed dorm. . . . He said, 'Hey, man, what are you doing?'" And then Beau separated the guy from the woman.

Joe continued: "He [Beau] ended up paying a price, because this guy [the groper] was the captain of a particular team, and the word went out, *Get Biden.* . . . [But] they didn't count on Beau Biden's little brother," Joe said, and then, for the first time in the speech, he smiled and flashed those pearly whites. "He came up and beat the hell out of the captain." The crowd laughed. "You think I'm joking? I'm not joking."

Classic Biden values: *The Biden clan sticks together.* Joe had always placed family above all else, and he passed the lesson on to his sons. "The first memory I have is of lying in a hospital bed next to my brother," Hunter said, fighting back emotion, when speaking at Beau's funeral. "I was almost three years old, I remember my brother, who was one year and one day older than me, holding my hand, staring into my eyes, saying, 'I love you, I love you, I love you,' over and over and over again. And in the forty-two years since, he never stopped holding my hand, he never stopped telling me just how much he loves me. But mine wasn't the only hand Beau held. Beau's was the hand everyone reached for in their time of need, Beau's was the hand that was reaching for yours before you even had to ask."

Beau didn't just look out for his little brother; he protected his father, too. After Joe Biden's 2012 debate against Paul Ryan, some critics said he "laughed too much." Well, Beau would have none of that non-sense, rushing to the morning shows to defend his old man: "Anytime folks on the far right are going after my father for smiling too much, that's a victory," Beau said. "My father spoke clearly to the American people about the facts. He did that for ninety minutes straight. This is not about how much my father smiled. . . . It's about talking directly to the American people about very important facts."

But as strongly as Beau protected the Biden name, he didn't want to use it as a crutch. Obama told a story about how in his twenties, Beau was stopped for speeding outside of Scranton. "The officer recognized the name on the license, and because he was a fan of Joe's work with law enforcement, he wanted to let Beau off with a warning," said Obama. "But Beau made him write that ticket. Beau didn't trade on his name."

When he joined the National Guard and then served overseas in Iraq, he feared getting special treatment because of his famous father, so he requested the Biden name tag be stripped from his uniform. (As Joe later remembered, he used a fake name instead, something like "Roberts.")

"He abhorred people who had a sense of entitlement, and he went the other way," Joe later said of his son. "He won the Bronze Star and came home, and made us all promise that we *wouldn't tell anybody* that he won the Bronze Star." When he was awarded the Legion of Merit, he wouldn't put it on his uniform until his general ordered him to.

And in a generational echo of Joe's playfulness, Beau had a lighter side, too. "When he'd have to attend a fancy fund-raiser with people who took themselves way too seriously, he'd walk over to you and whisper something wildly inappropriate in your ear," Obama remembered, laughing a bit. At Thanksgiving, he was known to dance in a sombrero and shorts, just to get a laugh out of his family. For Halloween he once dressed as Don Johnson in *Miami Vice*, all decked out in a white jacket and shoes with no socks.

That upbeat personality of Beau's, if he wanted, could have easily glided into the U.S. Senate. For thirty-six years, Joe Biden had a steel grip on his Delaware seat. When he became vice president, many assumed that the old seat would go to the heir apparent, his son. It would be so simple. Beau was the attorney general, making him perfectly qualified to step in and fill his father's shoes. The governor offered to appoint him to the vacant seat—no election, no fund-raising, no muss, no fuss.

Beau turned it down.

He already had a job, as attorney general, and he wanted to finish his work. "I have a duty to fulfill as attorney general," he said at the time, "and the immediate need to focus on a case of great consequence. And that is what I must do." Specifically, he was spearheading the case against a child molester; to Beau, it was more important that he mete out justice than accelerate his personal career. As Obama put it, "He didn't cut corners."

And he did his job well—he fought to imprison people guilty of child sex crimes, notching 180 convictions. "Nothing is more important than keeping our kids safe," Beau wrote in an op-ed. "No one likes talking about pedophilia and predators who want to hurt our kids, but we have no choice. . . . As adults, we all have a responsibility to protect children and take action when we believe a child is being abused." This sounds, in other words, like the son of the man who had passed the Violence Against Women Act.

===

IN 2010, WHILE IN THE best shape of his life—and after serving overseas in Iraq—Beau went for a ten-mile run. He collapsed from a stroke, was taken to the hospital, and was later diagnosed with stage 4 glioblastoma cancer in the brain. As with his father before him, they cut into his head. He had surgery. Chemo. Radiation.

In 2013, a small lesion was removed from his brain and then, briefly, he was given a clean bill of health and went back to work as attorney general. For a spell the cancer retreated. The Biden family fought it by banding together. And this time the Biden family included a new honorary member.

You know all the memes about how Obama and Biden were Best Friends Forever? Those memes hint at a deeper truth. As far too many families know, the costs of health care can be crushing. This is true even for the powerful families of DC. As Beau received cancer treatment, Joe knew that he might need to help with the costs. But after forty years as a public servant, he was long on love but short on cash. (Way back in 1972, as that brash twenty-nine-year-old, he'd vowed that "I'll never own a stock, bond, or debenture as long as I'm in public life." He kept that promise.) If things got any worse, the only way to make ends meet would be to sell the house.

Then Joe received an offer of financial assistance from a man who had become like a brother: Barack Obama. As Biden remembers it, Obama told him, "Don't sell that house. Promise me you won't sell the house. I'll give you the money. Whatever you need, I'll give you the money. Don't, Joe—promise me. Promise me."

And then another promise was requested—this time from his son. During what must have been agonizing cancer treatment, Beau seemed more concerned about how *others* were doing, not about his own pain. "Dad, I know how much you love me. Promise me you're going to be all right," he told Joe. His very last words to Joe were to soothe. "Dad, I'm not afraid. Promise me you'll be all right."

Remember home base.

Beau lost his fight against cancer on May 30, 2015.

Delaware lowered its flags to half-mast. "Beau measured himself as a husband, father, son, and brother. His absolute honor made him a role model for our family," Joe said when his son passed. "Beau embodied my father's saying that a parent knows success when his child turns out better than he did. In the words of the Biden family: Beau Biden was, quite simply, the finest man any of us have ever known."

Obama gave the eulogy at Beau's funeral. "From his dad, he learned how to get back up when life knocked him down," Obama said. "He learned that he was no higher than anybody else, and no lower than anybody else—something Joe got from his mom, by the way. And he learned how to make everybody else feel like we matter, because his dad taught him that everybody matters."

We can't pretend to understand the grief that flooded through Joe Biden, but we can admire the way that he carried himself with strength, dignity, and grace. He allowed us just a glimpse of the pain on an unforgettable appearance on *The Late Show with Stephen Colbert*.

The segment started much like any late-night segment. With the 2016 election looming in the background—and with Joe yet to declare—Colbert gently asked him, "Do you have anything you'd like to tell us?"

"Yes," Biden said, not missing a beat. "I think you should run for president again, and I'll be your vice president."

In hindsight, a 2016 matchup of Trump versus Biden is now one of the most enthralling what-ifs in American history. The conventional wisdom is that Democrats did not "connect with the working class"; Biden always has. Biden is authentic. And in this world where the U.S.

president has bragged about sexual assault, suddenly Biden's gaffes, by comparison, seem as harmless as using the wrong salad fork. "That's the biggest tragedy in the last election," says his old foreign policy guy, Mike Haltzel, adding that Biden would have "trounced Trump."

Yet it was not to be. Even putting aside the issue of whether Biden could have edged out Clinton in the primary, he explained to Colbert why he couldn't do it. Not then. Not so soon after Beau. "I don't think any man or woman should run for president unless, number one, they know exactly why they would want to be president, and two, they can look at folks out there and say, 'I promise you have my whole heart, my whole soul, my energy, and my passion,'" Biden said. "And, I'd be lying if I said that I knew I was there. I'm being completely honest."

And in one of the *realest* moments ever broadcast on television, Joe opened up about his grief. "Sometimes it just sort of overwhelms you," he said, and then showed just one more reason why we love him. He deflects the attention, he doesn't make it about him, and instead he thinks about the grief of others. "[There are] so many people who have losses as severe, or maybe worse, than mine, and don't have the support I have," he said.

These aren't just words. Joe decided to back up that sentiment with action. Every year, roughly fifteen thousand men and women die from brain cancer. *Enough*, Biden said.

Flash forward to Obama's final State of the Union. "Last year, Vice President Biden said that with a new moonshot, America can cure cancer," Obama said. "Tonight, I'm announcing a new national effort to get it done. And because he's gone to the mat for all of us, on so many issues over the past forty years, I'm putting Joe in charge of Mission Control. For the loved ones we've all lost, for the family we can still save, let's make America the country that cures cancer once and for all."

The Cancer Moonshot would be more than symbolic. And Biden would do more than just lend his name and prestige. He put himself to work. In June 2016, he unveiled the federal Genomic Data Commons—a database for consolidating all the key clinical trials, stats, and treatments. He gave a speech to the world's largest cancer conference, about thirty thousand medical professionals. "Imagine if you all worked together," he said. And as the crowd laughed he added, "I'm not joking."

He's not joking and he's not quitting. Joe Biden doesn't give up easily. He didn't give up on conquering his stutter. He didn't give up on the Violence Against Women Act. He didn't give up on Bosnia.

Biden keeps fighting, and he remembers the words and the values of his son. Those values sustain him. In 2011, Beau gave a commencement address at his old alma mater, Syracuse Law School. "You'll find peace when there are certain rules that are not malleable," Beau said. "Your conscience, your conscience should not be malleable. Your values ... These are the things that will guide you. They'll also be the things to save you."

WISDOM OF BEAU

Your values guide you. Your values save you.

Get Back Up! (2016—Forever)

*"Millions of Americans have been knocked down,
and this is the time [when] we get back up,
get back up together."*

IN THE FADING TWILIGHT OF the Obama administration, just days before the inauguration of you-know-who, Biden was summoned to a meeting with the president. Turns out it was something of a news conference—and Joe was the surprise star.

"I don't want to embarrass the guy," Obama began, as the room started to laugh.

And then he embarrassed the guy. Biden stood there, trying to keep a poker face—a tall order for Biden, even in the best of circumstances—as Obama sang his praises, called him "my brother," and deemed him "the best vice president America's ever had." And in a self-aware nod to the thousands of memes, Obama also noted that "this also gives the Internet one last chance to talk about our bromance."

When Obama announced the true purpose of this surprise

ceremony—the awarding of the Presidential Medal of Freedom with Distinction—Biden spun from the cameras, then pulled out a handkerchief to wipe the tears that gushed down his cheeks.

As Obama explained, the last three presidents had bestowed this honor on only three other individuals: Colin Powell, Ronald Reagan, and Pope John Paul II. A mix of honorable, hopeful, and Catholic—very Biden.

You've seen clips of the footage, but it's worth revisiting the moment in a bit of slow motion, as it does encapsulate, in a sense, Biden's remarkable journey. Obama said that in the eight years since he'd first tapped Biden as VP, "There has not been a single moment since that time that I have doubted the wisdom of that decision. ... This is an extraordinary man, with an extraordinary career in public service."

Some quick highlights from the citation:

In a career of public service spanning nearly half a century, Vice President Joseph R. Biden Jr. has left his mark on almost every part of our nation. ...

Let those words sink in—*nearly half a century*. When Biden first hopped on this roller coaster, the number one issue was the war in Vietnam.

Fighting for a stronger middle class, a fairer judicial system, and a smarter foreign policy, providing unyielding support for our troops, combating crime and violence against women, leading our quest to cure cancer, and safeguarding the landmark American Recovery and Reinvestment Act from corruption.

True, true, true, true, and true.

With his charm, candor, unabashed optimism, and deep and abiding patriotism, Joe Biden has garnered the respect and esteem of colleagues of both parties.

Who else is so beloved on both sides of the aisle? As Biden once said, "Let's get something straight right off the bat. I don't like John Boehner. I *love* him."

After the reading of the citation, Joe leaned in to kiss Jill, then Hunter, then Ashley. Obama stepped behind Biden, gave him a pat on the shoulders, and tenderly placed the ribbon around his neck, as tears poured down Biden's cheeks. The two men hugged.

The moment was touching, genuine, and spawned a billion tweets and gifs. A quick sampling:

JOE: "I am the watcher on the wall."
BARACK: "No, it's not that."
JOE: "I pledge my life and honor to the Night's Watch."
BARACK: "Okay, 'winter is coming.'"

JOE: "I've . . . haaaaad the time of my lifffe."
BARACK: Joe, chill.
JOE: C'mon, 8 years.
BARACK: Fine.
JOE: "And I've never felt this way before. . . ."

JOE: In the brightest day, in darkest night, no evil shall—
BARACK: This doesn't make you Green Lantern, Joe.

There's one more thing Obama said in that Medal of Freedom ceremony, a bit that got lost in the tsunami of tweets and jokes:

"The best part is, he's nowhere close to finished," Obama said. "In the years ahead as a citizen, he will continue to build on that legacy internationally and domestically. He's got a voice of vision and reason and optimism and love for people, and we're gonna need that—that spirit and that vision, as we continue to try to make our world safer, and to make sure that everybody's got a fair shot in this country."

And that's exactly what Joe has been doing. He did not let the election of Donald Trump cripple his spirit. He did not stop fighting for his values. And he has not remained silent. How could he? He's Joe Biden.

For starters, as counterintuitive as this sounds, he is actively pulling for Trump, because he sees that as pulling for America. "I give you my word as a Biden. I've been rooting for his success," he said in June 2017. "It's desperately in all of our interest to do that. And if you notice, Barack and I have not gone after him personally. We've not gone into that mosh pit." (Let's quickly pause to savor the visual of Joe and Barack, body-slamming each other in a mosh pit.) "We have taken issue with him when we think he's wrong," he quickly clarified, "which is, to be very blunt about it, most of the time."

Remember how in 1972, Joe Biden refused to run any negative ads against Caleb Boggs, no matter how gentle? Those values have stood the test of politics, setbacks, and heartache.

Yet that doesn't mean he's shy about sticking up for the values that he cherishes about our country, especially when he sees them under siege. In reaction to the Muslim ban and the Mexico border wall, Biden spoke out against what he called "hate speech" and "fringe ideologies." He has defended the Affordable Care Act, calling John Mc-

Cain before a crucial repeal vote, urging him to vote against the repeal. (McCain listened.) He advised Trump to "Stop tweeting."

Respect and #resist—not mutually exclusive.

Biden's post-2016 priorities also serve as a useful reminder that life—and even activism—is about more than just presidential politics. He reminds us that no matter who's in the White House, no matter who controls Congress, and no matter who wears the robes on the Supreme Court, there are things that all of us can do, in our own lives, to support the values we believe in. *Fight for the little guy. It takes a small man to hit a small child.* These principles have shaped his career, and they continue to guide him as he steps up his efforts to stop sexual assault on campus, building on the work that he began in the early '90s, with the Violence Against Women Act.

He's visiting campuses. Giving speeches. And he has a blunt message for the men out there, the ones who might dismiss sexual assault as a "women's issue." *Malarkey.* Everybody can do something. "But it's up to all of you to have the gumption to stand up and speak out," he says. "Don't look left and right. Look in the mirror."

Biden is a good reminder that no matter what we're doing, it's important to focus on the people, the personalities. "A good life at its core is about being personal," he once said. "It's about being engaged. It's about being there for a friend or a colleague when they're injured or in an accident, remembering the birthdays, congratulating them on their marriage, celebrating the birth of their child. . . . It's about *loving someone more than yourself.* . . . It all seems to get down to being personal."

Joe has the whole "loving someone more than yourself" thing covered. Just look at him and his wife. Still in love, still gooey, still holding hands more than forty years after he saw that poster of her in the airport. At the 2017 Tonys, Joe tagged along as Jill's plus-one. (*Hi, I'm Joe, Jill's husband.*) As she gave a speech to introduce a performance, Joe, smitten, turned to the producer and said, his voice thick with emotion, "That's my wife." (At the same show, incidentally, his chair broke, and he tried to fix the chair himself, as a Secret Service agent shined a flashlight.)

The Joe Biden story does not yet have a tidy ending. There are many unknowns. This book went to press in the autumn of 2017, so any speculation will soon be outdated . . . but what the hell, here's a thought: People might think of Biden as *too old* to run for president. (On inauguration day of 2021, Biden would be 78 years old, or nine years older than Reagan in 1981.) And yet. Back in 1972, people thought he was too young, at twenty-nine, to run for the Senate. Joe Biden has that Irish blood, that rebel spirit that made him run under dump trucks as a kid, throw water balloons, and sneak into a private hotel in the Bahamas. You have to wonder . . . since Biden launched his career with a campaign where "age is an issue," maybe he'd bookend that career with another campaign where age is an issue, and once again defy the odds?

Only one thing is certain. No matter what happens next, and no matter how bruising the challenge or heartbreaking the tragedy, Joe Biden will do what Joe Biden has always done: He will get back up. And now he's imploring *all of us* to raise our chins, to step forward, to come back from our own setbacks and tragedies, big and small, just as he has.

"Millions of Americans have been knocked down," Biden has said. "And this is the time [when] we get back up, back up together." Get back up from the political mat. Get back up from the loss of a job. Get back up from the crushing burden of student loans. Get back up from a romantic breakup. Get back up after the smaller setbacks in life, like missing your bus or the Amtrak. Another one will come. Wait for it. Smile. Hug a friend. Buy some ice cream. Take heart in the little things, the tiny moments, like when you're headed to the airport, and even though you're tired as a dog, you happen to see a group of Cub Scouts, so you give them a tour of your plane.

Just get back up.

ACKNOWLEDGMENTS

IT SHOULD NOT COME AS a surprise to hear that I've always been fond of Vice President Joe Biden. (The secret's out—I'm biased!) And as I dug in to research this book, and as I learned more details, context, and nuance about the way that he has lived his life with integrity, my appreciation only deepened.

So thank you, Vice President Biden, for (1) offering your service to the country, (2) living your life with such class and grace, and (3) enduring this silly book with good humor. (Vice President Biden did not ask for this book. He's a humble guy. I can imagine him rolling his eyes and saying, "That's a bunch of malarkey.") So thank you, sir, for taking this all in stride. And thank you to Dr. Jill Biden, the entire Biden clan, and all of Team Biden (such as Senator Ted Kaufman, Ron Klain, Tony Blinken, Tom Donilon, Jake Sullivan, and so many others) for all that you have done to support the Biden journey.

Thank you to my extraordinary agent, Rob Weisbach—Rob, I'm as crazy about you as Delaware is about Biden. (One day Rob asked me, "Hey, what do you think about Joe Biden?" Goose bumps. Thank you for the inspiration, Rob.) Huge thanks to my editor, Matt Inman, who is literally the only person on the planet I could imagine editing this book. Thanks, Matt, for asking all the tough questions, for the sharp eye, for saving me from myself, for the 3 a.m. editing sessions, and for the *Star Trek* joke.

Thanks to the incredible team at Three Rivers Press, including marketing aces Kathleen Quinlan and Julie Cepler, publicist extraordinaire Kathryn Santora, production manager Kevin Garcia, cover designer Alane Gianetti, interior designer Andrea Lau, production editor Craig Adams, and to everyone else behind the scenes for all their hard work.

It was a delight to speak with the folks in the Biden universe. Thank you to Arun Chaudhary, Herbie Ziskend, Victoria Nourse, John Marttila, and Mike Haltzel. Professor Laurence Tribe, thank you for sharing your stories about the Bork nomination. Thanks to former president of the National Organization of Women Patricia Ireland for the crucial context, and thanks, Branden Brooks, for sharing your story (and photos) with me. Thanks also to those who spoke with me on background.

Thanks to the brave souls who volunteered to read early drafts of the manuscript and provide valuable feedback. Huge thanks to Lisa Schiller for the hot-off-the-press reads, and for the many enthusiastic texts of encouragement. Thanks to Caitlin Moscatello (life-saver), Dolly Chugh (for the sharp notes and the unflagging support), Laura Brounstein (for the feedback and good vibes), Cody Dolan (the streak lives!), Rochelle Bilow (*traditions*), Terry Selucky, Shawn Regruto, Ben Bowman, Joe Hall, Josh Wilbur, Jen Doll, Catherine Perez, Tania Hoff, Trevor Hoff, and Sarah Murray (thanks, Sis!). Thank you, all of you.

Thanks to my parents, stepparents, sisters and brother, cousins, aunts, and uncles. Thanks to the Wednesday Night Writer's Group. To the Paragraph writer's space. To the lifelong Texas/FFL gang (and spouses and kids!) of Eric Pedersen, Chris Shaver, Todd Rinaldo, Dan

Abbruscato, Walker Robinson, James Mangano, Trevor Hoff, Tania Hoff, Charlie Applegate, and Joe Hall.

Thanks, as always, to Keith Meatto, Jamie Davis, Evan Aronowitz, Curtis Sparrer, Leo Lopez, Paul Jarrett, Laura Demoreuille, Lee Bob Black, Adam Smith, Matt Smith, Kabir Merchant, Erik Brown, Teddy Vuong, Omer Mohammed, Dave Spinks, Stephane Conte, and Wes Hollomon. To my old coauthor and good friend Andrea Syrtash, to Amy Braunschweiger, Brian Sack, Stephanie Meyers, Elizabeth Meggs (sorry there's not more about Biden pets!), Erica Ho, Katherine Conaway, Meghan Miller, Christine, and to Allison Joy of Comstock's. To Megan Lynch *(Alles Gute, immer)*.

A big thanks as always, of course, to Michael Sang, Betsy Poris, Judy Newman, Juliet Nuss, Harry McNeill (I finally learned how to spell your name!), Xiaodi Qu, Traci Swain, Ann-Marie Resnick, Ellie Chamberland, Wayne Friedman, Mike White, and the rest of the mighty crew at Scholastic. (I miss you guys already.)

Oh, one more bit of thanks? To President Barack Obama. Sir, you made a good choice.

ENDNOTES

A QUICK NOTE ON NOTES:

As this is not a scholarly or academic work, I wanted to avoid bogging the reader down with in-text citations and footnotes. Yet it's important to attribute sources (part of the Wisdom of Joe, see Chapter 5), so I've done my best, in the following pages, to show where each quote is drawn from.

Broadly speaking, there are four buckets of sources for this book: (1) my interviews with people who knew or worked with Joe Biden; (2) books about Biden; (3) articles about Biden; and (4) the thousands and thousands of things he has said in speeches, interviews, and TV appearances.

Happily, Joe Biden has been in our lives for more than forty years, and with all that time in the public eye, he has given us a joyful amount of raw material. *The Book of Joe*, clearly, would not be possible without this mountain of quotations. (Am I the only one at 2 a.m. who watches old YouTube clips of the Bork hearings?)

The book also owes a huge debt to Jules Witcover's hustle and legwork in *Joe Biden: A Life of Trial and Redemption*; he uncovered so many great gems and anecdotes. (Thank you, sir.) For anyone who has caught the bug and wants a more comprehensive look at Biden's life, definitely check out Witcover. And the Biden chapters from Richard

Ben Cramer's classic, *What It Takes*, are absolutely top-notch. (The world lost Cramer to lung cancer in 2013. At the time, Vice President Biden said, "It is a powerful thing to read a book someone has written about you, and to find both the observations and criticisms so sharp and insightful that you learn something new and meaningful about yourself. That was my experience with Richard.")

I'm especially indebted to the blue chip reporting by Evan Osnos in *The New Yorker* (shout-out to "The Biden Agenda"), Glenn Thrush in Politico ("Joe Biden in Winter"), Steve Clemons in *The Atlantic* ("The Biden Doctrine"), Jeanne Marie Laskas in *GQ* ("Have You Heard the One About Joe Biden?"), John Richardson in *Esquire* ("Joe Biden, Advisor in Chief"), Mark Bowden in *The Atlantic* ("The Salesman"), George Packer in *The New Yorker* ("Washington Man," and of course Packer's book *The Unwinding*), and all of the tireless, underappreciated journalists at the *New York Times*, the *Washington Post*, and countless others.

And as the best person to comment on the insight of Joe Biden is, well, Joe Biden, I'm especially grateful for the anecdotes, perspective, and lessons he shares in *Promises to Keep*. It was a brave book for him to write, and much of what we know about his early life, especially the painful moments from 1972, we only really learned from that book. I can't recommend it enough for anyone who wants the more complete Joe Biden picture. (Thank you, Mr. Vice President.)

Okay, on to the nitty-gritty:

INTRODUCTION

xi   **Cub Scouts anecdote**—Herbie Ziskend phone interview, June 19, 2017, supplemented with contemporary TV coverage (such as CBS.com: http://www.cbsnews.com/news/cub-scouts-get-a-campaign-plane-tour-from-biden).

xii **"He's almost exactly the same."**—Arun Chaudhary phone interview, June 22, 2017.

xii **"Folks don't just feel"**—from the Medal of Freedom ceremony, January 12, 2017.

xiii **"If you can't admire Joe Biden"**—"Watch Lindsey Graham Choke Up Talking About Joe Biden," *Huffington Post*, July 2, 2015.

xiii **"Joe Biden doesn't have a mean bone"**—Laskas, "Have You Heard the One About President Joe Biden?"

xiii **"I've known eight presidents"**—August 22, 2012, https://www.youtube.com/watch?v=7c23RegP8lU.

xiv **"If you ask me"**—Biden has said the "luckiest/unluckiest man alive" quote many times; to cite two sources: "Speaking Freely, Biden Finds Influential Role," *New York Times*, March 28, 2009, as well as United States Senate Oral Histories Project, which supply the rest of the Ted Kaufman quotes that appear in this book, https://www.senate.gov/artandhistory/history/resources/pdf/Kaufman_Oral_History.pdf.

1

THE BOY WHO COULDN'T SPEAK (1942–60)

3 **"I may be Irish, but I'm not stupid."**—"The Best of Biden Being Biden from the New Congress' First Day," PBS.org, January 6, 2015.

3 The four-hour talking marathon was actually the night of Biden's aneurysm, as detailed in Richard Ben Cramer's *What It Takes*.

3 **"I talked like Morse code . . ."**—Osnos, "The Biden Agenda."

4 **"spunky Irish lass with a mind of her own"**—Jules Witcover's delightful description, from *Joe Biden: A Life of Trial and Redemption*. (For brevity, the rest of the citations of "Witcover" refer to this book.)

4 **"Nobody is better than you"**—Biden's speech at the 2008 Democratic National Convention, which is also the source for "it's because you're so bright you can't get the thoughts out quickly enough."

4 **His sister, Val**—Witcover.

5 **"Feat of the Dump Truck"**—Cramer, *What It Takes*.

5 **"Joe was just a daring guy"**—as told to Witcover.

6   **"You ca-ca-can't catch me!"**—"Joe Biden's Scranton Roots," *Times Tribune* (Scranton, Penn.), January 21, 2009.

6   **push-alert notifications from *Car and Driver***—Thrush, "Joe Biden in Winter."

6   **One year, the owner of his father's dealership**—story Biden has told many times.

6   **"When I got knocked down by guys"**—quote from Biden's 2008 Democratic National Convention speech.

7   **"Joe Impedimenta" nickname, kids in alphabetical order, Sir Walter Raleigh episode**—Cramer's *What It Takes*; 2011 essay Biden wrote for *People*.

9   **Mother driving him back to school, "rip that bonnet off"**—*Promises to Keep*.

9   **"My name is Joe Biden, and I love ice cream"**—"Vice President: 'My Name Is Joe Biden, and I Love Ice Cream,'" TheHill.com, May 18, 2016.

9   **"Find someone who looks at you like . . ."**—@mgargeya, https://twitter.com/mgargeya/status/859601036578783232

10   **"He gets excited about ice cream"**—Arun Chaudhary phone interview, June 22, 2017.

10   **Big Red, White & Biden:** http://www.pbs.org/newshour/art/heres-scoop-new-joe-biden-ice-cream-flavor/, May 31, 2017.

10   **Archmere, "my deepest desire, my Oz," and washing windows, etc.**—*Promises to Keep*.

12   **"When Joe sticks up for the little guy"**—President Obama's comments honoring Biden during the Medal of Freedom ceremony, January 12, 2017.

12   **Football and "Hands" anecdotes**—Witcover.

12   **"Biden . . . lugged the pigskin"**—*Chester Delaware County Daily Times*.

13   **Realizing that he liked public speaking**—*Promises to Keep*.

13   **"Mr. Walsh," he said**—Witcover.

14   **The Sweater Kid**—Branden Brooks phone interview, June 26, 2017.

2

HOT YOUNG BIDEN (1960–72)

18 **"I probably started my first year of college"**—*Promises to Keep.*

18 **"dated a lot of girls," thoughts of becoming a priest, advice from the headmaster**—Witcover.

18 **Hot Young Biden memes:**
@_naidacielo, https://twitter.com/_naidacielo/
status/797298666360819712
http://harryedward.tumblr.com/post/153113723249
@GalacticToasts, https://twitter.com/GalacticToasts/
status/793962011793170432.

19 **"a lot of new girls to meet," "luscious pink pile," "dozens of beautiful young college girls sunning themselves," Spring Break/ Bahamas anecdote**—summarized from *Promises to Keep* and Witcover, whose interviews with Biden's friend Fred Sears corroborate the coin-flip story.

21 **Yacht Man, accompanying dialogue, "ass over tin cup in love," and "You know we're going to get married"**—*Promises to Keep.*

22 **Biden and Booze**—"Biden Clenches Plastic Beer Cup in Teeth to Free Hands for Clapping," *The Onion*, January 28, 2014.

22 **"enough alcoholics in my family"**—2008 Biden interview with the *New York Times.*

22 **"Joe would do wild and crazy things . . ."**—Witcover.

22 **"I'm against chemical crutches"**—*Wilmington Journal*, November 11, 1970 (via Witcover).

24 **Quitting football and borrowing car to visit Neilia, car-ferrying scheme, "She wanted five . . ."**—*Promises to Keep.*

25 **"He's going to be a senator by age thirty"**—as Bobbie Greene McCarthy said to Witcover.

25 **Neilia's note on the windshield**—"The Bidens: 'Magical' Years as Newlyweds in Syracuse," *Syracuse Post-Standard*, May 31, 2002.

25 **Biden marrying Neilia in 1966**—Ibid.

26 **Joe Sr. giving the Corvette as a wedding gift**—as Biden shared on *Jay Leno's Garage*, https://youtu.be/mP-hyDSlmUs.

26　**Moving into 608 Stinard, the puppy "Senator"**—"The Bidens: 'Magical' Years as Newlyweds in Syracuse."

26　**Casual attitude toward law school, "sloppy and arrogant" student, brush with plagiarism, and accompanying quotes**—*Promises to Keep.*

27　**Biden cramming for finals with Neilia's help**—Ibid.

3

THE HAIL MARY (1972)

29　**"snowman's chance in August"**—*Promises to Keep.*

30　**"Well, who's going to be his campaign manager?"**—from the United States Senate Oral History Project (all Kaufman quotes are from the Oral History Project, later referred to as "Senate oral histories"), https://www.senate.gov/artandhistory/history/oral_history/KaufmanEdwardE.htm.

30　**Ted Kaufman riff and quotes, on the party leaders mentioning Joe and Val Biden**—Senate oral histories.

30　**Val's role in the first election**—both Witcover and *Promises to Keep.*

31　**Launching on March 20, 1972, flying in propeller plane**—Witcover.

31　**18 percent versus 93 percent name recognition**—Kelley, "Death and the All-American Boy."

31　**Coffee, "carried them from house to house"**—*Promises to Keep.*

32　**Asking for vote**—Herbie Ziskend phone interview, June 19, 2017.

32　**Inviting scholars to dinner on Sunday nights**—*Promises to Keep.*

32　**"These were issues that not a lot of elected officials"**—Senate oral histories.

33　**"malarkey"**—*Promises to Keep.*

35　**"He's just a very ethical guy"**—*Wilmington News*, October 2, 1972 (via Witcover).

35　**"a nice guy, but he's just not an innovative senator"**—Kelley, "Death and the All-American Boy."

35　**I LOVE CALE button anecdote**—Nancy Doyle Palmer, "Joe Biden: 'Everyone Calls Me Joe,'" *The Washingtonian*, February 1, 2009.

35 **"We produced some radio advertising"**—John Marttila phone interview, June 20, 2017.

35 **"stupid and a horrendous waste of time"**—*Promises to Keep*.

36 **"Hey, I'm going to vote for your dad!"**—Ibid.

36 **"You know, not since Henry Clay"**—Ibid. It's possible that Biden's reading of history wasn't 100 percent accurate, as in 1818, John Henry Eaton was sworn in to the Senate at age twenty-eight, and in 1934, Rush Holt Sr., like Biden, turned thirty after his election to the Senate.

36 **Hopping out of the car at red lights, wedding crashing, winning the Jewish vote**—Witcover.

36 **"Energizer Bunny"**—Witcover.

37 **F. Nordy Hoffman anecdote, quotes**—Senate oral histories, https://www.senate.gov/artandhistory/history/oral_history/F_Nordy_Hoffman.htm.

38 **"Joe the Lifeguard"**—story and all quotes (prior to 2017) as shared by Biden in *Promises to Keep*.

39 **"I owe you all"**—"Joe Biden Recalls Lessons Learned as the Only White Lifeguard at City Pool in 1962," *Washington Post*, June 27, 2017.

40 **Biden's grocery store radio ads, Val quotes**—"Biden's Road to Senate Took Tragic Turn," NPR, October 8, 2007, as well as *Promises to Keep*, corroborated by Marttila phone interview.

40 **Description of brochures, Chris Matthews quotes**—"Who Joe Biden Was When We Met Him Is Who You See Now," MSNBC.com, June 1, 2015.

41 **"Biden post office"**—as told in *Promises to Keep*, Marttila phone interview, F. Nordy Hoffman via Senate oral histories.

41 **debate night anecdote, quotes**—"The Family Man Takes a Leap," *Chicago Tribune*, August 14, 1987.

42 **"clubbing the family's favorite uncle"**—*Promises to Keep*.

42 **Boggs's kitchen sink attack ad**—Ibid.

42 **"I knew the answer I thought they wanted to hear," "Joe, I sure in hell hope"**—*Promises to Keep*.

43 **"You ran a good race, Joe," and his response**—Ibid.

43 **Kaufman memories of victory**—Senate oral histories.

43   **"I may go down and be the lousiest senator"**—*Wilmington News*, November 9, 1972 (via Witcover).

44   **2,500 staffer applicants**—*Promises to Keep*.

44   **Description of family cutting cake**—archival photo.

44   **Traveling to DC to buy a house, "exceeded all my romantic youthful imagining"**—*Promises to Keep*.

45   **"She's dead, isn't she?"**—2012 speech Biden gave to military families at the annual TAPS National Military Survivor Seminar, as well as *Promises to Keep* and "Joe Biden's Heartfelt Speech on Grief," *Washington Post*, May 31, 2015.

45   **Thoughts of suicide**—2012 speech to military families, "Joe Biden's Heartfelt Speech on Grief."

46   **Comments at Neilia's funeral**—*Wilmington Journal*, December 20, 1972 (via Witcover).

46   **"No words, no prayer, no sermon gave me ease," "bust out of the hospital"**—*Promises to Keep*.

46   **"Look, Joe, why don't you take a year"**—Witcover.

47   **"I'm going to jump right in there with you, son."**—"Senator-Elect's Wife Dies in Auto Accident," *Cedar Rapids Gazette*, December 19, 1972.

47   **"One of my earliest memories"**—Beau Biden's 2008 speech at the Democratic National Convention.

47   **Nixon, Biden audiotapes**—now publicly available, accessed via https://www.youtube.com/watch?v=lz2ofDFUlN4.

48   **"There will come a day, I promise you"**—2012 speech to military families, "Joe Biden's Heartfelt Speech on Grief."

49   **"Caring about your colleague"**—2017 commencement speech at Colby College (Waterville, Me.), "Joe Biden Explains How This One Trait Can Make You Both Happy and Successful," CNBC.com, May 23, 2017.

49   **Mike Mansfield "six months" anecdote, and Biden's insistence on commuting every day via Amtrak**—*Promises to Keep*.

50   **Hägar the Horrible**—Fussman, "Joe Biden: What I've Learned."

50   **"I'm going to shove my rosary down their throat"**—Sullivan, "Does Biden Have a Catholic Problem?"

50   **"I find great solace in my faith," set of rosaries, "I will wear it till I die"**—NPR *Fresh Air*, June 15, 2017.

51   **Beau Biden wearing a sweater under a blazer, resting on a hospital bed**—archival photo.

51   **"I hope that I can be a good senator for you all"**—*Wilmington News*, January 6, 1973 (via Witcover).

51   **Val moving in to look after the boys, Biden leading them in prayers**—*Promises to Keep*.

4
BIDEN TIME (1972–88)

55   **"I ain't changing my brand . . ."**—Thrush, "Joe Biden in Winter."

55   **As a rookie senator, Neilia's ring on his finger**—*Promises to Keep*.

56   **a rule for Beau and Hunter, "wild card"**—*Promises to Keep*.

56   **"We have an expression"**—D'Agostino, "Things My Father Taught Me."

56   **Kissinger anecdote, accompanying quotations**—*Promises to Keep*.

57   **Seeing old senators naked**—Ibid.

57   **"We were walking the street late at night" in New Orleans**—*Wilmington Journal*, January 3, 1974 (via Witcover).

58   **"It seems to me that we should flat-out tell the American people"**—Kelley, "Death and the All-American Boy."

58   **"The voters of Delaware who elected this stupid"**—"Joe McQuaid's Publisher's Notebook: Biden, Mercier Said It Well," UnionLeader.com, November 27, 2011.

58   **Public financing idea, "youngest *one-term* senator"**—*Promises to Keep*.

59   **Helms once wrote, "Crime rates"**—"Thunder from the Right," *New York Times Magazine*, February 8, 1981.

59   **Mike Mansfield anecdote**—Biden's commencement speech at Yale University (New Haven, Conn.), May 17, 2015, https://obamawhitehouse.archives.gov/the-press-office/2015/05/17/remarks-vice-president-yale-university-class-day; also appears in *Promises to Keep*.

60   **"look past the caricatures"**—Biden's commencement speech at Yale.

60   **"Every time there's a crisis in the Congress"**—Ibid.

60   **Strom Thurmond, "Segregation in the South"**—"Thurmond's Support of Daughter Varied," *Washington Post*, December 23, 2003.

61   **"Strom Thurmond was" and the rest of "Biden and the Capacity for Change" sidebar**—Biden's eulogy for Strom Thurmond, http://www.americanrhetoric.com/speeches/joebidenstromthurmondeulogy.htm.

62   **"I'd be a damn liar"**—*TV News: The People Paper*, September 26, 1974 (via Witcover).

62   **"I want to make sure"**—Ibid.

62   **Purse-rescuing anecdote**—"Though Small in Size, Delaware Big on Biden," *USA Today*, October 9, 2008.

63   **"If it's ever a choice"**—Mike Haltzel phone interview, June 21, 2017.

63   **Seeing Jill's poster in the airport, "blonde and gorgeous"**—*Promises to Keep*, other public mentions.

63   **Meet-cute anecdote and dialogue**—as shared in *Promises to Keep*.

64   **"I was really charmed by him"**—*Piers Morgan Tonight*, January 23, 2012.

65   **"She had that way of looking at you"**—Cramer, *What It Takes*. (Technically, Cramer's book is not a "biography" but a sprawling account of the '88 election, yet his sections on Biden are so thorough and rich and well-researched, the word "biographer" feels appropriate.)

65   **meeting the families**—*Promises to Keep*.

65   **Beau and Hunter lobbying Joe to propose to Jill**—Ibid.

66   **Five marriage proposals, the ultimatum, "I'm not going to wait any longer," and finally yes**—Ibid.

67   **burgers at Blimpie's**—*Promises to Keep*, although, to be fair, it's unclear if Blimpie's ever served burgers.

67   **"I've had two moms"**—Beau Biden's interview with Ann Curry, *Today*, August 27, 2008, https://archives.nbclearn.com/portal/site/k-12/flatview?cuecard=35906.

5

BIDEN V. BORK (1987–88)

68   **"Judge Bork, I guarantee you this little mallet"**—Senate hearings.

68   **"It's time we hear the sound"**—"Biden: Something About '88 Keeps Beckoning," *New York Times*, December 19, 1985.

68   **"I'm not going to run in 1988"**—Witcover.

69   **"Although no one questions Biden's ability"**—"Biden Struggles with Tragedy in '88 Decision," *Los Angeles Times*, February 8, 1987.

69   Reagan's **"No man in America"**—"Consider Bork's Merit, Not His Ideology, Reagan Asks," *Los Angeles Times*, July 30, 1987.

70   **Kennedy's epic anti-Bork quote**—public record (accessed NPR.com, December 19, 2012).

70   **"We will fight it all the way—until hell freezes over"**—NAACP Executive Director Benjamin Hooks, quoted in "NAACP Hears More Voices Against Bork," *Chicago Tribune*, July 7, 1987.

70   **George Will quote**—*Washington Post*, July 2, 1987.

71   **Ted Kaufman quote**—Senate oral histories.

71   **"Overwhelming prospect" he would oppose Bork**—"Biden Plans to Oppose Bork," *Washington Post*, July 9, 1987.

71   **"the biggest mistake of my political career"**—Gitenstein, *Matters of Principle* (via Witcover).

71   **The seemingly going back-and-forth about whether he supports Bork**—Witcover.

72   **Biden doing his homework**—as he shares in *Promises to Keep*, and as corroborated by email exchange with Professor Laurence Tribe (June 28, 2017).

72   **"The Book of Bork" as name of compendium**—Witcover.

73   *Griswold v. Connecticut* **analogy**—*National Lampoon's National Vacation.*

74   **Kaufman's "We were doing very well"**—Senate oral histories.

74   **Biden liking the Kinnock quote, deciding to use it**—*Promises to Keep.*

75   **Summary of the debate, forgetting to credit**—Cramer, *What It Takes*; Witcover; *Promises to Keep.*

76   **DEBATE FINALE: AN ECHO FROM ABROAD**—*New York Times*, September 12, 1987.

77   **"Plagiarizing Joe"**—"Eminently Qualified Bork Victim of Unfair Attack Attempting to Distort Record," *New York Times*, September 15, 1987; *Promises to Keep*.

77   **"This controversy plays"**—"Biden Was Accused of Plagiarism in Law School," *New York Times*, September 17, 1987.

77   **Actual headaches**—Cramer, *What It Takes*; Witcover; *Promises to Keep*.

77   **"I guarantee you this little mallet"**—Bronner, *Battle for Justice*.

78   **"rush over to Bork's water glass"**—Ibid.

78   **"We must also pass judgment on whether"**—Bork hearings public record.

78   **Back and forth on Biden v. Bork**—from hearings public record, with insights on strategy from *Promises to Keep*.

79   **Role play and "mock hearing"**—Tribe email, June 28, 2017.

81   **"higher IQ than you do"**—archived C-SPAN video from 1988's "Road to the White House," accessed via, https://www.youtube.com/watch?v=D1j0FS0Z6ho.

81   **"only one in my class"**—Witcover.

81   **"Mr. Biden is a gentleman of high moral character"**—Cramer, *What It Takes*.

81   **"Of all the things to attack you on," "It was my fault"**—*Promises to Keep*.

82   **"Hello, everybody"**—Cramer, *What It Takes*; *Promises to Keep*.

83   **"You have to win this thing!"**—*Promises to Keep*.

83   **Jimmy Carter**—*Promises to Keep*.

83   **Fund-raising**—Connaughton, *The Payoff*.

84   **Paul Ryan**—"Joe Biden's Alpha-male Display Leaves Paul Ryan Overwhelmed in VP Debate," *The Guardian*, October 12, 2012.

84   **Donald Trump**—"Biden Blasts Trump: 'I Wish I Could Take Him Behind the Gym," TheHill.com, October 21, 2016.

85   **Kaufman**—Senate oral histories.

85 **"Unenumerated and unarticulated rights . . . ," follow-up dialogue**— Senate hearing official records, also Witcover and *Promises to Keep*.

86 **"Anything else you want to say, Judge Bork?"**—Senate hearings.

86 **Bottles of champagne, "There's nothing here to celebrate"**—*Promises to Keep*.

87 **"acquitted himself superbly"**—*Legal Times*, December 1987 (via Witcover).

87 **"instructed all of us"**— Gitenstein, *Matters of Principle* (citing *New York Times* column by Anthony Lewis).

87 **Biden's (amazing!) chat with Reagan**—*Promises to Keep*.

88 **"Joe Biden played a more consequential role"**—Toobin, "Biden and the Supreme Court."

88 **"I have no real doubt"**—Tribe email, June 28, 2017.

89 **At gym thinking it was a muscle pull**—Cramer, *What It Takes*; *Promises to Keep*.

89 **"think you're too arrogant" exchange**—as relayed by Ted Kaufman in Senate oral histories.

89 **Talking for hours . . . he blacked out**—Cramer, *What It Takes*.

89 **Thoughts after he woke up**—*Promises to Keep*.

90 **"a spa for Valentine's Day"**—Cramer, *What It Takes*.

90 **Drama of the hospital**—big debt here to Cramer's gripping account in *What It Takes*.

90 **"Doc, what are my chances?" and dialogue**—story Biden has shared publicly, this dialogue from his 2013 speech at the White House National Conference on Mental Health, via CNSNews.com June 5, 2013.

92 **"I've asked you all to come today"**—*Promises to Keep*.

93 **"What a smart guy!"**—Witcover.

94 **"Good news is that I can do anything I did before"**—Margaret Carlson, "Biden Is Also Reborn," *Time*, September 12, 1988.

6

IT'S ON US (1988–94)

95 **"You're a coward for raising a hand to a woman or child"**—Biden, "20 Years of Change: Joe Biden on the Violence Against Women Act."

95 **Montreal Massacre**—"The Montreal Massacre: Canada's Feminists Remember," *The Guardian*, December 3, 2012.

96 **"victim's race, ethnicity, religion, or sexual orientation"**—The Supreme Court clerk was Lisa Heinzerling. She wrote an article that Ron Klain, a top Biden aide, gave to then-Senator Biden. "Ladies' Man," *New Republic*, September 23, 2008.

96 **He found appalling statistics**—*Promises to Keep*.

96 **"He wanted to hear what women had to say about it"**—Phone interview with Victoria Nourse, July 14, 2017.

97 **"The stupidity was infuriating"**—*Promises to Keep*.

97 **"Damn it, when you get married"**—Bronner, *Battle for Justice*.

97 **Goldfarb, "lack of control that is experienced"**—"Ladies' Man," *New Republic*, September 23, 2008.

98 **"Well, Judge" and Thomas / Biden exchange**—Senate records.

98 *Karate Kid* **"crane kick" analysis**—my own demented mind.

98 **"You will be pleased to know"**—Senate records.

98 **"Biden's queries were sometimes"**—Mayer and Abramson, *Strange Justice* (via Witcover).

99 **Specter's recollections of Thomas denials**—Arlen Specter, *A Passion for Truth* (via Witcover).

100 **"for this Senator, there is no question"**—Terkel, "Joe Biden Is a Hero Among Women's Rights Groups. But It Wasn't Always That Way."

100 **"I must start off with a presumption"**—Senate records.

101 **Mikulski, "What disturbs me"**—Terkel, "Joe Biden Is a Hero Among Women's Rights Groups. But It Wasn't Always That Way."

102 **Strom Thurmond, Clarence Thomas, and Anita Hill quotes**—Senate records; Hill, *Speaking Truth to Power*.

102 **"half the senators on Capitol Hill"**—Mayer and Abramson, *Strange Justice*.

103 **Biden not admitting lie detector test**—"Effect of Hill's Taking of Lie Test Uncertain," *Los Angeles Times*, October 14, 1991.

103 **"myth . . . that we somehow denied her"**—Witcover.

103 **Biden's letter inviting Angela Wright to testify**—Terkel, "Joe Biden Is a Hero Among Women's Rights Groups. But It Wasn't Always That Way," an overall excellent piece that gives good context.

103 **"I wanted a panel on sexual harassment"**—Ibid.

104 **"I think he did two things that were a disservice to me"**—2014 interview on HuffPost Live.

104 **"Then-Senator Biden felt that he had an obligation"**—Dovere, "Biden's 'Anita' Problem."

105 **"There is absolutely not one shred of evidence to suggest that Professor Hill is fantasizing"**—Senate records.

105 **"I am no longer an anonymous, private individual"**—Hill, *Speaking Truth to Power*.

105 **In 1991, Patricia Ireland**—Patricia Ireland phone interview, July 21, 2017.

106 **"The country changed"**—Nourse phone interview, July 14, 2017.

106 ***Violence Against Women: A Week in the Life of America***—from the report, accessed via http://library.niwap.org/wp-content/uploads/2015/VAWA-Lghist-SenateJudiciary-10.92.pdf.

107 **"Everyone knew that it was *personal* for him"**—Nourse phone interview, July 14, 2017.

108 **"the one person most responsible for passage of this bill"**—"Biden Savors a Hard-fought Victory," *The News Journal from Wilmington, Delaware*, August 26, 1994.

109 **"When I look at Biden and the Anita Hill hearings"**—Ireland phone interview.

7

SECOND CHANCES (1991–2008)

111   *"And I absolutely can say, with certainty"*—Nicole Gaudiano interview of Biden, August 26, 2007 (via Witcover).

111   **"Mr. Walsh, I want"**—Witcover.

111   **2 million miles on Amtrak**—"Joe Biden Gets Bipartisan Tribute on the Senate Floor," *Los Angeles Times*, February 1, 2017.

111   **"I've met with virtually every leader"**—"8 Times Joe Biden Sounded Like a Presidential Candidate (Even Though He Isn't One)," ABCNews .com, September 8, 2015.

112   **Averell Harriman's advice**—*Promises to Keep.*

112   **He learned of mutilations, beatings**—Ibid.

112   **"The West has dithered so pathetically"**—Biden, "More U.N. Appeasement in Bosnia."

113   **"Biden opposed Clinton on Bosnia"**—Mike Haltzel phone interview, June 21, 2017.

113   **Milošević "war criminal" anecdote**—story Biden has told on campaign trail and in debates.

113   **"When you look back"**—"Biden Played Less Than Key Role in Bosnia Legislation," *Washington Post*, October 7, 2008. (As you might guess from the title, the article also makes the point that Biden was far from the only reason the United States took action.)

114   **Joe the Name-Butcherer**—Haltzel phone interview, June 21, 2017.

115   **NATO expansion**—Ibid.

117   **"He would greet the vice president"**—Arun Chaudhary phone interview, June 22, 2017.

118   **Alexander Hamilton quote**—(Forgive me, *I couldn't resist.*) Senate records.

118   **"If the president successfully prosecutes the war"**—Witcover.

119   **"too much of a long shot"**—"Sen. Biden not running for president," CNN.com, August 12, 2003.

119   **"I don't think John Edwards knows what the heck he is talking**

about"—"A Biden Problem: Foot in Mouth," ABCNews.com, January 31, 2007.

120 **"I'd be a little surprised if he actually does run"; Obama's on "every-one's number-two list"**—Witcover.

120 **Kaufman quotes**—Senate oral histories.

121 **"The bottom line is that"**—"Biden Stumbles in Interview," *Washington Post*, October 25, 2007.

121 **"articulate and bright and clean"**—"Biden Unbound, Lays into Clinton, Obama, Edwards," *New York Observer*, February 5, 2007.

122 **Ezra Klein "Bye Bye Biden"**—title of his blog post on *The American Prospect*, January 31, 2007.

122 **Trying to explain "clean" and "articulate"**—*The Daily Show*, January 2007.

122 **"I didn't take Senator Biden's comments personally"**—official statement from Obama, January 31, 2007.

123 **Iran/Pakistan debate**—Technically the three candidates did not say "Iran," "Iran," "Iran," back to back to back, of course; this is a touch of dramatization, but that's basically the gist.

123 **"With a failing economy"**—Former CIA station chief of Islamabad, Kevin Hulbert, "Falling Economy and Rising Nuke Arsenal Make Pakistan the Most Dangerous Country for World, Claims Former CIA Official," *The Indian Express*, February 16, 2017.

123 **Kaufman quotes**—Senate oral histories.

124 **"giving Iowa voters full paragraphs"**—*Pittsburgh Post-Gazette*, December 29, 2007 (via Witcover).

125 **"nothing to be sad about tonight"**—transcript of caucus speech, http://p2008.org/biden/biden010308spt.html.

125 **Shermanesque comments**—Nicole Gaudiano interview of Biden, August 26, 2007 (via Witcover).

126 **"If you win," "Be careful" back and forth**—Lizza, "Biden's Brief."

126 **Obama's "I am more concerned and interested"**—Plouffe, *The Audacity to Win*.

126 **"Bill may be too big a complication"**—Ibid.

126   **"We knew Biden could be somewhat long-winded"**—Witcover.

126   **The "secret meeting" and quotes**—Plouffe, *The Audacity to Win*.

127   **Obama and Biden tête-á-tête**—"Biden's Unified Theory of Biden," *Newsweek*, October 3, 2008.

128   **"picking me for my judgment"**—*ABC's The Week*, December 21, 2008.

128   **"This baby just needs a little scrub down"**—"Shirtless Biden Washes Trans Am in White House Driveway," *The Onion*, May 5, 2009.

129   **Muscle cars**—Phillips, "What I'd Do Differently: Vice President Joe Biden."

129   **"My fondest memory"**—D'Agostino, "Things My Father Taught Me."

130   **"I know [Joe] as an incredible father"**—Beau's unforgettable speech at the 2008 Democratic National Convention.

8

FROM GAFFES TO GLORY (2008–2016)

135   **"The number one issue facing the middle class [is] a three-letter word: Jobs. J-O-B-S"**—"Oh, That Joe! (No. 29 in a Series)—Obama & Biden's Three-Letter Word: J-O-B-S," ABCNews.com, October 15, 2008.

135   **"when the stock market crashed"**—Biden to Katie Couric, September 23, 2008.

135   **"It will not be six months before the world tests Barack Obama"**—to a roomful of donors, via CNN.com, October 20, 2008, http://www.cnn.com/TRANSCRIPTS/0810/20/ldt.01.html.

135   **Clinton "might have been a better pick"**—"The Caucus," *New York Times*, September 10, 2008.

136   **"you cannot go to a 7-Eleven . . . unless you have a slight Indian accent"**—Biden actually said this back in 2006. This is one of those quotes, like many, that sound far more damning out of context. The C-SPAN show *Road to the White House* showed a clip of Biden saying that he has strong support among Indian-Americans, partly because Delaware has a strong Indian-American community. The full quote: "I've had a great relationship. In Delaware, the largest growth in population is Indian-Americans moving from India. You cannot go to a 7-Eleven or a Dunkin' Donuts unless you have a slight Indian accent. I'm not joking." After the blowback, Biden's office (via Margaret Aitken) clarified:

"The point Senator Biden was making is that there has been a vibrant Indian-American community in Delaware for decades. It has primarily been made up of engineers, scientists and physicians, but more recently, middle-class families are moving into Delaware and purchasing family-run small businesses."—Associated Press, July 7, 2006.

136   **"Stand up, Chuck!"**—(Oof.) Accessed via, https://www.youtube.com/watch?v=C2mzbuRgnI4.

136   **"a chill set in"**—Heilemann and Halperin, *Game Change.*

137   **"At first, people would complain"**—Arun Chaudhary phone interview, June 22, 2017.

137   **"He's doing endless pushups"**—Herbie Ziskend phone interview, June 19, 2017.

137   **"He just kept holding up vials of liquid"**—Chaudhary phone interview, June 22, 2017.

138   **Beau and Hunter staying with Joe after debate prep, "Remember, remember home base"**—as Biden shared after receiving the Medal of Freedom. The full quote: "You heard that the preparation for the two debates—vice presidential debates that I had—I only had two that Beau and Hunt would be the last people in the room. And Beau would say, look at me, Dad. Look at me. Remember, remember home base. Remember." Accessed via https://www.bostonglobe.com/news/politics/2017/01/12/read-full-remarks-from-biden-send-off/j8zyBJsh63IehZaDQuaaFJ/story.html.

138   **"My goal tonight was a simple one"**—*Saturday Night Live*, October 5, 2008.

139   **Biden helping to persuade Clinton to accept role of secretary of state**—Witcover.

139   **"I love you, darling" to Clinton**—Osnos, "The Biden Agenda."

140   **Maureen Dowd quote**—"Oval Newlywed Game," *New York Times*, February 14, 2009.

140   **"Biden felt insulted"**—Bailey, "Joe Biden, White House Truth Teller."

141   **"Are we winning today?"**—Ziskend phone interview, June 19, 2017.

142   **Aaron Burr dig**—Again, I couldn't help it. (Old habits . . .)

142   **Choosing between the VP archetypes, considering Quayle an ideologue**—hat tip to the indomitable Jules Witcover.

142   **Favorite VP as Dan Quayle because of swimming pool**—"Joe Biden's Favorite Veep? Dan Quayle," CBSNews.com, April 12, 2010.

143   **"Every single solitary appointment"**—"Biden to Head New Middle-Class Task Force," Politico.com, December 21, 2008.

143   *Joe, you do Iraq*—Osnos, "The Biden Agenda."

144   **The plan for more settlements "undermines the trust," late for dinner date**—"Palestinians Complain to Biden About Settlement Plan," Reuters, March 10, 2010.

144   **"Few American politicians would think it wise to invoke crucifixion"**—"Netanyahu Sees Strike on Iran's Nukes as Worth the Risk," Bloomberg.com, March 26, 2012.

144   **"most succinct understanding"**—Osnos, "The Biden Agenda."

144   **"He has known Netanyahu"**—Ziskend phone interview, June 19, 2017.

145   **"They'll give me a line"**—Osnos, "The Biden Agenda."

145   **"This personal element"**—Clemons, "The Biden Doctrine."

145   **The legendary encounter with Putin**—Osnos, "The Biden Agenda."

146   **"In the midst of that debate"**—Ibid.

146   **Biden grilling the Situation Room about Pakistan**—Bailey, "Joe Biden, White House Truth Teller."

147   **"Joe is very good about sometimes articulating"**—"Speaking Freely, Biden Finds Influential Role," *New York Times*, March 28, 2009.

147   **Support for gay marriage**—*Meet the Press*, May 6, 2012.

148   **Biden and Memes:**
hid all the pens—@Barack_and_Joe, https://twitter.com/Barack_and_Joe/status/821852063332204547
knuckle sandwiches—http://knowyourmeme.com/photos/1190806-prankster-joe-biden
defeating ISIS—@Barack_and_Joe, https://twitter.com/Barack_and_Joe/status/797880493978984448
pizza order—@SavageJoeBiden, https://twitter.com/SavageJoeBiden/status/802699218737475584
fake birth certificate—@JonnySun, https://twitter.com/jonnysun/status/797198272079298568
Ashley's "He sat there for an hour and laughed"—Moneyish.com, March

13, 2017, https://moneyish.com/ish/this-is-joe-bidens-favorite-obama-biden-bromance-meme/
"Doesn't this feel right"—@TheDiLLon1, https://twitter.com/TheDiLLon1/status/788114505624612864.

149 **Biden's courtship of Arlen Specter**—"Biden Worked on Specter '100 Days,'" Politico.com, April 28, 2009.

150 **"This is a big fucking deal"**—I mean, it was.

150 **"last hope"**—"Biden Talks Seen as Last Hope for Debt Ceiling," Reuters, May 23, 2011.

150 **"close working relationship"**—"Biden, McConnell and the Making of a Deal," Politico.com, August 2, 2011.

150 **"We got results that would not have been possible"**—"Senators Deliver Farewell Tribute to Vice President Joe Biden," NPR, December 7, 2016.

151 **Biden's material at the Gridiron Club**—"Biden Lampoons Obama at Gridiron Dinner: 'He Thinks Easter Is About Him,'" *Huffington Post*, May 25, 2011.

151 **"Isn't it a bitch, this vice president thing?"**—"All Politics Is Personal," *Harvard Gazette*, October 3, 2014.

152 **"lubricated" joke**—YouTube, via *The Weekly Standard*, March 21, 2012.

152 **"His mom . . . God rest her soul"**—via YouTube.

152 **"largest economic stimulus in history"**—"Here's What a Biden Campaign Would Look Like," Politico.com, February 18, 2016.

153 **"But then he started drilling me"**—Ziskend phone interview, June 19, 2017.

153 **"As corny as it sounds"**—"Biden on July Fourth: Swearing in troops, cursing 'S.O.B.' Saddam," CNN.com, July 4, 2009.

153 **"Biden shook every hand"**—Traub, "After Cheney."

154 **swearing-in ceremonies**—"Biden Charms in Senate Ceremonies," TheHill.com, January 6, 2015.

154 **Valentine's Day windows stunt**—*ABC News*, February 12, 2010.

154 **rat on podium, overhead compartment**—Ziskend phone interview, June 19, 2017.

155 **April Fool's**—*Rachael Ray*, August 10, 2015.

155   **Obama, "first Second Lady in our nation's history to keep her day job"**—from speech awarding Biden with Medal of Freedom.

155   **sleeping with a community college professor**—"Joe Biden: I Sleep with a Cutie College Professor Every Night," CBSNews.com, April 7, 2014.

156   **"The absolute most important thing is your family"**—Ziskend phone interview, June 19, 2017.

156   **Letter to staff**—originally shared on Twitter via @DerekJJohnson— https://twitter.com/derekjjohnson/status/761603002406809600.

9
BEAU (1969–2015)

158   **"A parent knows success when"**—statement from VP Biden when Beau passed.

158   **"The incredible bond I have with my children"**—Biden's commencement speech at Yale University (New Haven, Conn.) on May 17, 2015; "Family Losses Frame Vice President Biden's Career," *Washington Post*, May 31, 2015.

159   **"He even looked and sounded like Joe"**—from Obama's eulogy honoring Beau Biden.

159   **"He didn't want any special attention"**—*The Late Show with Stephen Colbert*, September 10, 2015.

159   **"win it fair and square"**—Obama's eulogy honoring Beau Biden.

159   **"Biden Most Popular Man in Delaware—Beau"**—Biden's commencement speech at Yale University.

160   **"My son stepped in" comments**—"Joe Biden Speaks at Syracuse University About Sexual Assault Prevention," *The Daily Orange*, November 12, 2015.

160   **"The first memory I have is of lying in a hospital bed"**—Hunter's comments at Beau's funeral.

161   **"Anytime folks on the far right are going after my father"**—Beau Biden on *This Week*, October 14, 2012.

161   **Obama's story of Beau asking for the ticket**—Obama's eulogy.

161   **Fake name instead . . . like "Roberts"**—Biden on Colbert's show, September 10, 2015.

161   **"He abhorred people who had a sense of entitlement"**—Ibid.

161   **Beau's lighter side**—Obama's eulogy.

162   **Dressing up as Don Johnson**—"Beau's friends gather to recall a side of him few knew," DelawareOnline.com, June 6, 2015.

162   **"I have a duty to fulfill as attorney general"**—"Biden's Son Will Not Run for Father's Senate Seat," *New York Times*, January 25, 2010.

162   **"He didn't cut corners"**—Obama's eulogy.

162   **"Nothing is more important than keeping our kids safe."**—Beau Biden, "Shining a brighter light on child sexual abuse in Delaware," DelawareOnline.com, July 26, 2014.

163   **He collapsed . . . stage 4 glioblastoma cancer**—diagnosed in 2013, http://www.cancersupportcommunity.org/blog/2017/05/brain-tumor-awareness-month-cancer-research-and.

163   **Clean bill of health**—"Family Losses Frame Vice President Biden's Career."

163   **"I'll never own a stock"**—D'Agostino, "Things My Father Taught Me."

163   **"Don't sell that house"**—Biden interview with Gloria Borger, CNN, January 12, 2016.

163   **"Promise me you're going to be all right"**—Biden on Colbert's show, September 10, 2015.

164   **"Beau measured himself as a husband, father, son, and brother"**—statement released from VP Biden when Beau passed.

164   **"From his dad, he learned how to get back up when life knocked him down"**—Obama's eulogy.

164   **Colbert and Biden back-and-forth**—Biden on Colbert's show, September 10, 2015.

165   **"That's the biggest tragedy in the last election"**—Mike Haltzel phone interview, June 21, 2017.

165   **"I don't think any man or woman should run for president unless"**—Biden on Colbert's show, September 10, 2015.

165   **"Sometimes it just sort of overwhelms you"**—Ibid.

166   **"Imagine if you all worked together"**—"Joe Biden Just Announced a Huge New National Cancer Database," Fortune.com, June 6, 2016.

166   **"You'll find peace when there are certain rules"**—as Joe Biden remembered the speech (he quoted Beau when giving a commencement speech to Notre Dame, South Bend, Ind., in 2016), https://www.youtube.com/watch?v=gH99Ol7nTsY.

10
GET BACK UP! (2016–FOREVER)

167   **"Millions of Americans have been knocked down"**—from Biden's acceptance speech in 2008, which still seems as timely as ever . . .

167   **"I don't want to embarrass the guy"**—from the awarding of the Presidential Medal of Freedom ceremony.

169   **The memes:**
I am the watcher on the wall—@JillBidenVeep (parody account), https://twitter.com/JillBidenVeep/status/820297312412909568
I've . . . haaaaad the time of my life (this still cracks me up)—@TrentFromTwitta, https://twitter.com/TrentFromTwitta/status/819704201110581249
Green Lantern—@Barack_and_Joe, https://twitter.com/Barack_and_Joe/status/822174063653167104.

170   **"everybody's got a fair shot"**—from the awarding of the Presidential Medal of Freedom ceremony.

170   **"I've been rooting for [Trump's] success"**—NPR *Fresh Air*, June 15, 2017.

170   **Lobbying McCain before the health care vote**—"Biden Lobbied McCain on Healthcare Vote: Report," TheHill.com, July 29, 2017.

171   **"But it's up to all of you to have the gumption"**—"Joe Biden Speaks at Syracuse University About Sexual Assault Prevention," *The Daily Orange*, November 12, 2015.

171   **"A good life at its core is about being personal"**—Biden's commencement speech at Yale University.

172   **Biden at the Tonys**—"Joe Biden Tried to Fix His Broken Seat at the Tonys," *Page Six*, June 12, 2017.

SELECTED BIBLIOGRAPHY

Bailey, Holly. "Joe Biden, White House Truth Teller." *Newsweek*, October 9, 2009.

Biden, Joseph R. "More U.N. Appeasement in Bosnia." *New York Times*, June 7, 1993.

———. "20 Years of Change: Joe Biden on the Violence Against Women Act." *Time*, September 10, 2014.

———. *Promises to Keep: On Life and Politics.* New York: Random House, 2007.

Bronner, Ethan. *Battle for Justice, How the Bork Nomination Shook America.* New York: Union Square Press, 2007.

Clemons, Steve. "The Biden Doctrine." *The Atlantic*, August 22, 2016.

Connaughton, Jeff. *The Payoff: Why Wall Street Always Wins.* Westport, Conn.: Prospecta Press, 2012.

Cramer, Richard Ben. *What It Takes: The Way to the White House.* New York: Vintage Books, 1993.

D'Agostino, Ryan. "Things My Father Taught Me: An Interview with Joe and Hunter Biden." *Popular Mechanics*, May 18, 2016.

Dovere, Edward-Isaac. "Biden's 'Anita' Problem." Politico.com, September 21, 2015.

Fussman, Cal. "Joe Biden: What I've Learned." *Esquire*, December 14, 2011.

Gitenstein, Mark. *Matters of Principle: An Insider's Account of America's Rejection of Robert Bork's Nomination to the Supreme Court.* New York: Simon & Schuster, 1992.

Heilemann, John, and Mark Halperin. *Game Change: Obama and the Clintons, McCain and Palin, and the Race of a Lifetime.* New York: HarperCollins, 2010.

Hill, Anita. *Speaking Truth to Power.* New York: Doubleday, 1997.

Kelley, Kitty. "Death and the All-American Boy." *The Washingtonian*, June 1, 1974.

Laskas, Jeanne Marie. "Have You Heard the One About President Joe Biden?" *GQ*, July 18, 2013.

Lizza, Ryan. "Biden's Brief." *The New Yorker.* October 20, 2008.

Mayer, Jane, and Jill Abramson. *Strange Justice: The Selling of Clarence Thomas.* Boston: Houghton Mifflin, 1994.

Naylor, Brian. "Biden's Road to Senate Took Tragic Turn." NPR, October 8, 2007.

Osnos, Evan. "The Biden Agenda." *The New Yorker*, July 28, 2014.

Phillips, John. "What I'd Do Differently: Vice President Joe Biden." *Car and Driver*, September 2011.

Plouffe, David. *The Audacity to Win: The Inside Story and Lessons of Barack Obama's Historic Victory.* New York: Viking, 2009.

Sullivan, Amy. "Does Biden Have a Catholic Problem?" *Time*, September 13, 2008.

Terkel, Amanda. "Joe Biden Is a Hero Among Women's Rights Groups. But It Wasn't Always That Way." *Huffington Post*, January 12, 2017.

Thrush, Glenn. "Joe Biden in Winter." Politico.com, March 2014.

Toobin, Jeffrey. "Biden and the Supreme Court." *The New Yorker*, October 13, 2015.

Traub, James. "After Cheney." *The New York Times Magazine.* November 24, 2009.

Witcover, Jules. *Joe Biden: A Life of Trial and Redemption.* New York: HarperCollins, 2010.

ABOUT THE AUTHOR

JEFF WILSER is the author of six books, including *Alexander Hamilton's Guide to Life* and *The Good News About What's Bad for You . . . and The Bad News About What's Good for You*, named by Amazon as one of the Best Books of the Month in both Nonfiction and Humor. His work has appeared in print or online at *GQ, Esquire, Time, New York* magazine, *Glamour, Cosmo, mental_floss,* MTV, and the *Huffington Post*. His advice has been syndicated to a network of two hundred newspapers including the *Miami Herald* and the *Chicago Tribune*. He grew up in Texas, used to live in New York, and is now traveling the world indefinitely. Twitter at @JeffWilser.